WHAT GERMANY FORGOT

THE MACMILLAN COMPANY
NEW YORK · BOSTON · CHICAGO · DALLAS
ATLANTA · SAN FRANCISCO

MACMILLAN AND CO., Limited
LONDON · BOMBAY · CALCUTTA · MADRAS
MELBOURNE

THE MACMILLAN COMPANY
OF CANADA, Limited
TORONTO

JAMES T. SHOTWELL

WHAT
GERMANY FORGOT

THE MACMILLAN COMPANY
New York •1940

Copyright, 1940, by
THE MACMILLAN COMPANY.

Set up and printed. Published January, 1940.
Reprinted May, 1940

PRINTED IN THE UNITED STATES OF AMERICA

PREFACE

This book was begun as an introduction to a volume *The Cost of the World War to the Central Powers*, by Dr. Leo Grebler and Professor Wilhelm Winkler, which is a statistical summary of conclusions drawn chiefly from the *Economic and Social History of the World War* [1] and published as a supplement to that series. The issues which it raised with reference to Germany, however, were too far-reaching to be covered within the limited space of a prefactory statement, especially as they have acquired an even greater importance, with the outbreak of the present war, than in the years of liquidation after the World War. In the survey which follows, some of the more important of these issues are reviewed in the light of many long-term researches in different countries which have opened up a different perspective from that widely accepted, not only in Germany but in America as well. It is to be expected that the conclusions here presented will be unacceptable to those who have unconsciously but effectively aided the cause of militarism in the post-war years by putting all blame for what has happened upon the Treaty of Versailles. This book is not a defence of that Treaty, of sections of which the author has been critical both during and after the Peace Conference; [2] but it is a reminder that wholesale denunciation of the peace

[1] Published in the United States by the Yale University Press (150 volumes, 1921–1937). See below, Chapter VIII.

[2] Reference is made to my diary and comments made at the time *At the Paris Peace Conference* (New York, MacMillan, 1937).

settlement of 1919 has served a political purpose which is the very opposite of what American liberals — who have accepted it as a dogma — have set forth as their ideal. It is a strange but unhappy paradox that liberalism, by instinct sympathetic to lost causes, can be more easily taken off its guard than reactionary conservatism which is by nature sure of itself. But true liberalism has this great advantage, that it has an open mind. To those — and there are many — who are now moved to re-examine the bases of their opinions, this book is offered for the light it may throw upon the background of the history of our time in which the forces of destiny are now moving on an obscure but tragic course.

In the preparation of this volume the author is under obligation to two collaborators with the Division of Economics and History of the Carnegie Endowment for International Peace, Mr. Alexander Gourvitch, who analyzed the material in the German volumes in connection with the publication of Professor Mendelssohn-Bartholdy's monograph, and to Mr. Sanford Schwarz, at present a member of the Division, whose assistance has been most helpful both in checking the data of research and in putting the volume through the press; and to the *New York Times*, which has given permission to reprint the greater part of Chapter I, which appeared as an article in the *New York Times Magazine*, November 5, 1939.

J. T. S.

CONTENTS

CHAPTER I

WHAT GERMANY FORGOT

THE Treaty of Versailles is still alive. By the strangest of paradoxes, the more Hitler insists that it is dead, the more surely it remains the issue in the diplomatic war which is just beginning. What England and France — and most other countries — regard as aggression is, in the eyes of Nazi Germany, a liberation from the "servitude" of 1919 permitting room to live and expand. The heart of the conflict, however, is something much more fundamental than the adjustment of frontiers; it is how people are to live behind the frontiers, and what kind of neighbors they will be. A settlement which accepted the German method of seeking redress, by the threat of war or the use of it, would fasten the clamp of new servitudes on the world of nations. That is what Hitlerism means to peace-loving democracies. It is a fact, however, of which Germany is largely unaware, due to the fact that the Treaty not only supplied a slogan of attack for the future but dominated — and distorted — the perspective of history as well. Just how this came about is worth careful study at this time.

The Treaty cost the German people more than the loss of territory or the weight of reparations; it distorted and falsified their view of history and their judgments of other nations. In fighting the Treaty, the German people transferred their whole attention to it, and by what seemed at the time a supreme effort of the will, forgot or ignored the effect of the World War itself. All the evils which the country suffered in the post-war years were attributed to the machinations of diplomats and statesmen after the soldiers' work was over. It was almost an article of faith that but for the Treaty Germany could have recovered speedily from the losses of the War. But no one knew what the War, as distinct from the Treaty, had cost it, and no one tried seriously to find out what proportion of the difficulties of the post-war period was chargeable to the account of each. Thus, as the process of treaty revision proved discouragingly slow, those who preached the resort to politics for power were able to carry the day.

The belief that the calamities of Germany were due to the Peace and not to the War was reinforced by nation-wide organized propaganda. I recall one incident which is typical. In the midst of the great inflation of 1923 when money was worthless, when one paid two billion marks for a postage stamp, there appeared in the store windows of towns and cities this printed sign, "The high price of the goods in this window is due to the 'Diktat von Versailles.'" The sign, printed in huge letters, was flanked by goods marked with astronomical figures in billions of marks. As the eye wandered over the articles which no one could buy back to the flaring headlines that put all the blame upon the Peace Treaty, one's memory of even the war-time hardships was submerged in a new and unforgettable experience. Imagine what this meant to the thrifty German housewife who tried to convert the falling marks of her husband's wages into goods and found them utterly beyond her reach. It is doubtful if any people in history ever was given such an object lesson. No wonder that the nation as a whole turned upon the Treaty of Versailles as the predominant if not the sole cause of its economic distress.

Moreover, the Treaty was something that might still be got rid of. The War was over and nothing could be done about it. The obligations which it left in Government debts and private losses had never been set forth in the clear-cut terms of a business statement; they were already confused with other things. Loans never quite ceased to look like investments. On the other hand, the Treaty presented a clear-cut statement of obligations for the present and the future. There, therefore, seemed to be just one thing for sensible Germans to do, and that was to concentrate their attention upon it with all the intelligence and vigor of a great people. That is what they did.

Any other nation in the same circumstances would probably have acted much the same way. But the effect of thus turning away from the cost of the War to the cost of the peace turned out in the long run to be one of the chief causes of Germany's undoing. It justified militarism and discounted, and later vilified, the processes of democracy. For there lay behind the German action a history and a trend of thinking which accepted war as the instrument of the nation's policy, and therefore justified its costs and sacrifices as a normal process of European political evolution. It was an attitude of mind which had been enforced by all the lessons of Prussian history and exemplified in heroic measure by Frederick the Great and Bismarck. The War therefore followed a great tradition, and the hardships it imposed were to be borne as a counterpart of the fighting. Yet for this military tradition of the nation in arms to be maintained after the terrific pressure of the World War, it was necessary that the hardships should not have been totally unbearable. It was at this point that the Treaty of Versailles became, by an almost miraculous paradox, the instrument for saving German militarism, by blinding the nation to the true nature of war when fought under the conditions of modern history and applied science. Everything could be blamed upon the peace terms. The only sufferings from the War were those of the past.

This transference of interest from the War that had been fought to the Treaty which was still to be got rid of did not begin immediately after the ratification of the Treaty of Versailles, however strongly the German nation reacted against its treatment. The memory of the sufferings of war-time were still too keen in the minds of everyone. The War, which had turned into a blockade of the Central Powers, had brought privation and even the threat of starvation to the mass of the German civilian population. It had indeed become a siege, a test of endurance, which continued throughout the winter of 1919 until the Armistice became a definite surrender. This had brought the War into every German home, leaving the scars of privation and suffering upon the German mind; and for a year or two after the Peace that memory was dominant.

But it is not humanly possible for either a nation or an individual recovering from illness to retain for more than a limited time the vivid and definite memory of past sufferings. Fortunately, the human system as it recovers health ceases even to be interested in past illness. This is especially true when new and pressing problems come to the fore, so that the mind cannot linger on the past even if it would. In the case of Germany the shift in interest began as soon as the Treaty of Peace was concluded, but it did not reach the proportions of a mental revolution until some time later. By the year 1922 the change in outlook practically gained the whole nation. The question of what the War had cost the country seemed by that time to be wholly unreal and academic compared with the pressing issue of the struggle to get rid of the burden of reparations.

This prodigious change in outlook was destined in the course of a few years to find its voice in the strident militancy of the Nazi movement, the first effect of which was to overthrow the Government of the Republic. But no one could foresee in the years immediately after the War that the protest against the Treaty could have any such sinister effect in Germany itself. After all, in turning its back upon the sufferings of war-time and directing its attention to present and future problems, Germany was only doing what the other countries of Europe were doing at that time. Not only did everyone, except a few historians, want to forget the nightmare through which Europe had passed, but common sense and pressing need led to a concentration upon problems of reconstruction. There was a world to rebuild, not only economically but physically as well. New nations had appeared on the map of Europe which had to be fitted into a new world system. Trade and commerce had to dig themselves new channels of intercourse where the old had been plugged or turned aside. Unrest and discontent were shared by capital, robbed of its income, and by labor suffering from unemployment. Thus the German tendency to forget the War was shared quite generally in other lands.

But while the tendency was general and was upon the whole a healthy sign of recovery it had no such fateful consequences elsewhere as in Germany. France had a constant reminder of war-time destruction in the devastated areas of the north; and even when it insisted most upon Reparation payments, they were not in themselves something new to be contrasted with war-time destruction, but simply a new embodiment of the damage caused by the War itself. They were a subtraction from, not an addition to, French war costs. In Germany the Reparation problem became more and more a thing apart from the War, a servitude that blocked the path and extinguished the hope of full recovery. In Great Britain the case was different; not only was the War deliberately forgotten, except for personal bereavement, but it was not long before Reparation too passed to the background as a disturbing factor in business, and British finance girded itself to face realities. This called for a frank acceptance of the War as the chief cause of dislocation of British credit and continuing unemployment.

Thus it happened that Germany, the nation that needed above all others in modern Europe to understand the nature of war, was the one which most definitely and positively turned away from it. In support of this movement a wholesale manipulation of history took place. The German army was represented as an ever-victorious force which had been "stabbed in the back" by Socialist plotters at home, a legend the falsity of which has been established by all sober historians and economists. The leaders of the revolution of 1918 and the founders of the German Republic were hounded from public life. Rathenau, the organizer of Germany's economic mobilization during the War, and Erzberger, the organizer of Reich finance at its close, were murdered by terrorist gangs. Suppressed militarism began its policy of violence in putsch uprisings, in one of which an Adolf Hitler escaped the bullets of the police by throwing himself on the pavement, and thus was saved for later things.

But it is more than a beer hall putsch which connects the Nazi movement with this concentration of German interest upon the Peace Treaty while ignoring or forgetting the burden which the War itself had placed upon the country. The Nazi movement has been throughout and still is a revolutionary movement, a fact which has been recently emphasized by the penetrating analysis of Dr. Rauschning in his *Revolution of Nihilism*. This means that it must always have a dissatisfied public opinion and some one or some thing to blame for whatever goes wrong. The fuel for such a revolutionary fire was abundant enough in post-war Germany. But no one could imagine laying the blame upon that militarism which was still regarded as having been a protector of the German home against foreign invasion. Any tendency to show up war as a technique of disaster was therefore all too likely to be regarded as unpatriotic. A much more obvious point of attack was the Peace Treaty, denounced by all parties, including those which reluctantly decided to fulfill its terms in the hope that thus they would be modified more quickly than any other way. By directing all attention upon the disastrous peace, foreign governments were made the conscious and continuing sources of Germany's ills.

It was but a step from this and one already inherent in the thinking of these revolutionaries, that those who dealt in high finance, especially the international bankers, among whom a number of Jews were prominent, should be regarded as the agents of this disaster.

How utterly mistaken all this has been should be apparent to anyone who looks back, not merely to the Treaty, but to the War behind it. For the total cost of the War to Germany was even greater than the "astronomical figures" finally summing up the arithmetic of reparation charges. It is true that no one can ever state positively, in the precise terms of arithmetic, how much a war like that of 1914–1918 costs any country. The only definite figures we have are those of the financial costs to the government, and they are open to criticism. In the case of Germany we do not have this for more than during the period of the war itself, but that alone was approximately 95 to 100 billion gold marks of the money of 1913; or double that amount if stated in the purchasing power of the mark of 1918–1919, which is the date at which the post-war economy had to be set going again. This does not include the continuing cost to the Reich in subsequent years which, as we know only too well from sad experience, rolls up like a snowball around the inner core of war-time expenses. Also it does not include the smaller but considerable costs to the governments of the various German states and municipalities. Nevertheless, even within these war-time limits it reached the appalling sum of something in the neighborhood of 50 billion dollars reckoned in money value at the close of the war.[1] How much more than this we should have to add in if we include the economic cost to the German people, is something that staggers the imagination. The ledgers of government accounts do not cover a nation's economy; beyond them lies the whole area of private industry, agriculture, and all the other activities of mankind, much of it moved from its very foundations by the giant forces of the World War. It would be a fair assumption that in exhaustion of human material and resources, deterioration of plant, capital displacement, and credit disturbance in what is perhaps the most highly industrialized country of the world, the economic cost of the War to the German people was probably

[1] See Dr. Leo Grebler, *The Effects of the World War on German Economy, especially German Industry* (Yale University Press, 1940) in *The Cost of the World War to the Central Powers.* This is a supplementary volume in the *Economic and Social History of the World War;* the other monograph in this volume by Professor Wilhelm Winkler, is *The Cost of the World War to Austria Hungary.* The volume is now in press. See the Preface of this volume.

as much, if not considerably more, than its cost to their Government. This would place the total financial and economic costs somewhere in the neighborhood of a hundred billion dollars. Had there been no Reparation or Treaty payments, Germany would still have had to meet as much of this vast economic cost and displacement as had not been met in war-time.

This, of course, does not mean that at the close of the War Germany was bankrupt to the extent of so many billion dollars. That would have rendered the Reparation Section of the Treaty of Versailles too absurd to be taken seriously. Much of the deficit was met at the time it was incurred by added effort, by self-denial and by exploitation of not only conquered territory but German resources as well. War-time economy is largely directed upon the task of making good as soon as possible what is destroyed or displaced. It also spreads the charges against the national economy of the future by loans and the use of credits. But the sum total of the account to be charged against the economy of war is not lessened by the fact that much of it is met before it reaches the stage of national bankruptcy. When we measure the costs of natural disasters, such as fire, flood or earthquake, we do not leave out of account what they cost us in money or effort during the catastrophe itself, any more than the loss of property on the part of the victims or expenses incurred and money spent by those working to rescue or restore. Similarly with war, the total cost includes much that is no longer visible when the war is over and much that is still to be calculated in the ledger of the future.

From what has just been said, it is clear that one of the reasons why Germany forgot the costs of the War and concentrated upon those of the Treaty, was that, while the latter were visible and present, the former were elusive and uncertain. But how elusive they were only those can appreciate who have tried to estimate or describe them.

Moreover, the literature on the subject, up to the last two or three years, has been singularly slight and superficial. The economists of the great classical period of the nineteenth century were frankly not interested in the complicated problem of war costs. This was partly a reflection of the optimism of the nineteenth century which, after the Napoleonic Wars, seemed to have opened an era in which steady progress toward peace was made through the lessening of the scope and frequency of wars. The accent, therefore, was on the processes of peace; war was regarded as a technique still necessary but receding slowly from the civilized world. This type of thinking continued even through the World War which seemed to deny its validity, and most recently has furnished support for the isolationist sentiment in the United States as expressed in the so-called Neutrality Legislation of 1937. It was in Nazi Germany and Fascist Italy that this traditional view of the decline and lessening place of war was first challenged. Recently a new literature has sprung up in these countries written in support of militaristic regimes, in which war is thrust back into the primary place it occupied in the savage world and economics is treated as its bond-servant.[2] Peace-loving peoples have found it hard

[2] Perhaps the most perfect statement of the militarist rejection of this idea of the decline of war with the progress of civilization was made by Signor Mussolini in his address to the Supreme Fascist Executive Committee on November 18, 1939. The press account quoted him as saying that the European war of 1939 had "already become a world war from a social and economic point of view"; and branding as "already academic" all pre-war discussion of economic problems and all talk of alleged differences between peace and war economics, he added: "There is only one

to take these ideas seriously; but the outbreak of the present
European war has at last begun to awaken their interest in
the subject. As yet, however, no Adam Smith of the economics of war has appeared.[3]

The difficulty seems to be that most people think in
terms of what they can see, such as the wreckage left by a
war or the restoration of the countryside, while the loss of
capital is not likely to be appreciated by anyone but the
loser. The best illustration of this fact is the over-powering
effect of the ravages of war in France upon the mind of
anyone who visited the occupied territories in 1919, over
against the destruction of private fortunes in time of inflation or depression. Yet the heaviest single register of
destruction in our time was to be found, not in the track
of devastating armies, but in that of the attack upon the
financial and economic structure of the nations at peace
in the Great Depression, which, in the economic history
of our times, was the last battle of the World War. Any
appraisal of what Germany suffered and endured, whether
from the War or the Treaty or both, can only be made in
the light of this universal experience of disaster. The

---

war economy because history shows that war is the normal state of
nations, at least those on the European continent. Those not recognizing
the fact that destiny and armed conflict must dominate economy must
not complain of the catastrophe toward which they are heading."

[3] Mention should be made of three works called out by the World
War: *The Political Economics of War* by Francis W. Hirst, 1915 (second
edition 1916); *The Economy and Finance of the War* (1916) and *The
Political Economy of War* (1921) by Professor A. C. Pigou. *The Economic and Social History of the World War* of the Carnegie Endowment presents a wealth of data which, as is pointed out elsewhere, has
not been fully used. Of the general literature on the subject the most
notable challenge to current ideas on war is that contained in the writings
of Sir Norman Angell, especially *The Great Illusion* (1910).

German literature on the subject of war economics has grown steadily
in recent years and however much its purpose may be suspect, it has
done something to clarify the problem by its analysis of the data.

problem is a much greater one than that of estimating the extent of the impact of the War upon Germany alone; for however much it may struggle to maintain itself as an autarky, it remains a part of the world economy.

This study does not attempt to follow the problem of war costs in all its intricacies. Its purpose is to bring it back to our minds so that we may have a clearer and more just understanding of other things as well. The present war in Europe is forcing the attention of all countries upon the experience of the past; and in no country was that experience more illuminating than in Germany. It would seem worth while, therefore, to recall the consequences of those years of titanic effort at mutual destruction in order to see better where we are today.

CHAPTER II

GERMAN WAR ECONOMY

In spite of the fact that the effect of the World War upon the German people has never been stated by German historians and economists with that competence and mastery of detail which has been the outstanding mark of German science, and that much of the source material is no longer available or has been destroyed, nevertheless enough is known of the way in which the war economy of Germany worked in various fields to offer the possibility of a fairly accurate reconstruction of this great page of its history. Some of the pertinent data, drawn for the most part from the German series of *The Economic and Social History of the World War*, have been summarized in the study by Dr. Grebler, to which the cautious student will probably wish to turn before accepting conclusions on the subject as a whole. But in the meantime it may be useful to have in mind a general outline of the character of German economy under the pressure of the War and the impact which it left upon German society.

The first and most familiar fact, one that is to be found in the opening pages of almost every German study of the World War, is that Germany was utterly unprepared for the way in which the War developed. This has been adduced to prove the innocence of German intentions in 1914; but it was equally true of all the other warring powers and proves nothing one way or the other with reference to war guilt. The only inference that can be

safely drawn from it is that the general staffs did not plan
for the kind of a war that developed after it had bogged
down to trench warfare on the front and to a blockade that
became a siege. The War of 1914 had been prepared for
according to the teachings of military experience in the
past with only such changes as were obviously called for
by the increased power of military machinery in both
armaments and transport. What happened was that the
war did not run true to form in the eyes of the most competent military specialists of the time, for nowhere else
was the conviction stronger than in Germany that the
War of 1914 would be a short one. The idea of the
Blitzkrieg, the lightning war, was not then, it is true, so
much a matter of faith as it became in the governing circles
of the Nazi with reference to the risk that they were taking
in the conquest of Poland and the earlier coups d'état.
Nevertheless, in 1914, Germany counted on a short war,
even when it had to be fought on both fronts. The Schlief-
fen plan for the invasion of France through Belgium was
accepted by the German Government in order to secure
a speedy decision by crushing France in a few weeks'
time. England could then be dealt with before it could
militarize its civilian population and Russia either held at
a distance or smashed before it had adequately mobilized.
The early weeks of the war seemed to be offering the
realization of this hope; even the retreat from the Marne
was neutralized by the battle of Tannenberg. During this
earlier period, therefore, there was no thought of the war
becoming a slow and exhausting siege, and no one dreamed
of the totalitarian war which was to involve the whole
civilian population of each of the warring nations.

The calculations of the General Staff seemed likely to
be justified at the opening of the war. It seemed to differ

from other wars not in kind but only in magnitude. The munitions industry, it is true, felt from the very first the stimulus of unprecedented production; but after all it was in a very real sense a part of the military machine. Similarly, if the progressive mechanization of the army, especially its motor transport system, led to a vast extension of the auxiliary services, the needs of the army in those opening months were not unlike those of German armies in the past, only larger, more varied, and more costly. The war itself was still regarded as a purely military affair; and if Germany did not hang out the sign "Business as Usual" as was the case in England, the confidence in the army and in the efficiency of the military supply system gave an initial sense of security under which business might be expected to suffer a minimum of disturbance.

Nevertheless, although the idea of a totalitarian war was still undreamed of, it was in the first month of the war and not in the latter period that business suffered a general paralysis. Unsold stocks accumulated on shelves and in warehouses. This was even true of the industry which was later to prosper most from the war, the Ruhr steel mills. The sudden dislocation of markets caused a stoppage in industry with resultant unemployment. As far back as 1907 Bebel, the great Socialist leader at the International Socialist Congress at Stuttgart, had foreseen this result when he opposed the general strike against war on the ground that "in wartime the workers will not demand a revolution, they will be clamoring for work and bread." Through the autumn months unemployment ran higher than had ever been known before. Even in December it was still three times as high as normal in winter months,[1]

---

[1] See Umbreit and Lorenz, *Die deutschen Gewerkschaften im Kriege* (Carnegie Endowment Series), p. 50 f.

and nearly twice as high as in the pre-war months. This continued into January. There was, therefore, much hardship in the opening weeks of the war, but the suffering was borne in a spirit of patriotic resignation, and the material losses entailed were accepted as temporary because of the confidence in a speedy victory. Moreover, private charity and public welfare measures relieved distress among the laboring classes.

By the end of the year, however, when the war had begun to show signs of longer duration, business began to revive. Already in the early months of 1915, the war "boom" had set in, which in one form or another continued through the succeeding years, down to the very period of the collapse. Business expanded to meet the appetite of war, and the greater that appetite the more it expanded. All the elements were present which make for the delusion of war prosperity as the national effort to meet the extraordinary demand was stimulated to a new and unprecedented extent. With the passing of unemployment in all but a few fields, there came a new and almost feverish demand for goods as those who were working at the great industry of destruction, War, earned higher wages. Had Germany been open to the markets of the world at this time, its government's control, effective as that was, could hardly have kept back the kind of inflation which played havoc with the costs of war materials to the Allies, forced to purchase them in foreign markets. Because it was thrown back upon itself by the blockade, the German wartime inflation could be kept easily within bounds and the dislocation of industry made to assume the appearance of a relatively controllable phenomenon.

The paradox grows when we find that the drift towards the war "boom" only set in in earnest after the battle of the

Marne had denied the hopes of an immediate victory and given a certain sense of permanency to war economy. As time passed, the very fact that the country was apparently refuting the theories of the economists that modern industrial society could not stand up under the strain of a long war, added to the continuing strength of the boom. Apparently industrial technique could be adapted to meet even such an emergency as this, and not only mass production but also the new processes of science substituted under the stimulus of war need for the slower methods of the past. Foreign economists like Professor Gustav Cassel of Sweden,[2] studying Germany's wartime experience, wrote glowingly of the "economic power of resistance inherent in a modern highly industrialized system," of its "elasticity," which without apparent economic disruption was able to take on such tremendous tasks in wholly new enterprises under handicaps which at first sight seemed utterly unsurmountable. This, however, proved to be an utter delusion.

The real measure of the transformation of German economic life due to war needs could only be taken when the stimulus to greater effort could be balanced against the strain which brought breakdown in both the human and the material resources of industry. This began to show itself at the very time when Professor Cassell was preaching the invincibility of the German war economy. It was in the long-drawn-out crisis of the battle of the Somme that Germany began to tighten its belt by the "Somme Program" for quickening army supplies. But disappointment followed and a more desperate effort had to be made. The result was the so-called Hindenburg Program of December, 1916, designed to meet new demands for

[2] Gustav Cassel, *Germany's Economic Power of Resistance*, Stockholm, 1916.

munitions not only by restrictions on the use of materials but the regimentation of civilian life so as to control and direct every energy of the nation towards fulfilling its wartime purpose.

Because of Germany's incomparable military establishment, by common agreement the best in the world in 1914, it is generally believed that she was better prepared for the World War than England and France. Although this was true from a purely military point of view, that is in armament and military competence, Germany began the war with an economic and financial structure that was ill prepared to meet the test of a long-drawn-out struggle. The almost miraculous expansion of her industries and commerce in the years preceding the war had weakened her financial structure by straining her credit to the full. The result was that when war came, in Germany the liquid capital available for war loans was less than it was in England or France. Even if it had been available, the tax system of the Empire was such as to make it almost impossible to provide for the increasing needs of war; for the Reich lacked a fiscal system of its own with which the fiscal administrations of Prussia and the other States could be brought in line. The result was the immediate issuance of paper money. It was on the afternoon of July 31, 1914, that the Reichsbank suspended payment of gold in exchange for its notes. Two billion paper marks were used for the expenses of mobilization and the first expenses of the war. During the war confidence in ultimate victory helped to maintain the value of this paper currency so that under the Imperial regime it never reached less than half its original value. But as the war wore on and the expenditure of the Reich reached the vast figures set forth in the pages below, the successive borrowings of the government from the banks on treasury bills, led unavoidably to more paper money and higher prices. The rise in prices which became so catastrophic two years after the war was over was already under way in wartime, and was only prevented from entering upon the vicious circle of high inflation by the solidarity of the German people under the pressure of war and the belief, shared by all, that in the end the enemy would be forced to foot the bill.

If the financial and credit situation in which Germany found itself at the opening of the war compared unfavorably with that of England or France, the trade situation was still worse because of the blockade. German ingenuity found many substitutes for the things it needed from overseas, but they were mostly dearer to make than to buy; and cut off from the world market, German industry was left with its own army as its best customer, a thoroughly wasteful system of internal economy. The customer, moreover, had insatiable demands which ultimately cost more than the combined military expenditures of England, France and Italy.

While Germany had not prepared itself in peacetime for the revolution in warfare which the World War brought with it, yet of all the warring countries it was the first to appreciate the changed character of warfare as the system of trenches stretched out from the Alps to the sea. Field guns and shrapnel gave way to a heavier artillery and high explosives. The demand for war materials pyramided. It is stated that the German army [3] fired more munitions in one day of battle in the World War than throughout the entire war of 1870–71, and that the weekly deliveries of gun barrels to the front equalled or exceeded the total

[3] *Cf.* Otto Goebel, *Deutsche Rohstoffswirtschaft im Weltkriege* (Carnegie Endowment Series), p. 19.

amount delivered in the former war. Such an expenditure of material in battle had never been planned or prepared. During the first six weeks of the war as much munitions had already been consumed as had been estimated to be enough for its whole duration. The General Staff and the munitions factories were able to keep their lead over the output of other countries because their plants were much more extensive and up to date. But when the sources of supply began to show signs of possible exhaustion, the General Staff had need of a new kind of mobilization, one which the military had never brought within their calculations. Industry had to be militarized throughout the entire nation if the supplies were to be kept adequate to wartime needs.

The one man who saw this first in all the world was Dr. Walther Rathenau. In August, 1914, Dr. Rathenau, the head of the great electric trust in Germany, the Allgemeine Elektrizitäts-Gesellschaft, had already pointed out to the war ministry the need for conserving the raw materials for munitions in view of the fact that so many of the German sources of supply would be cut off by the blockade. The war could then only be won by Germany mobilizing not only armies but industry as well. Instead of troops on the march and the clash of armies in the field he had a vision of tall chimneys pouring out smoke and of flaring furnaces lighting the sky all the way from Berlin to the Rhine. This, as he saw it, was the vital element in modern war. But mobilized industry meant mobilization of the sources of supply as well, for the whole structure of national defense under the conditions of modern science rests on raw materials.

Rathenau therefore proposed that there should be set up as a section of the war office an organization to deal with this matter of maintaining the supply of war materials. The proposal was not taken very seriously at the beginning, for he was supplied with only one assistant and a stenographic secretary and given a small room at the back of the War Office. He himself has left us a sketch of the way this little organization grew into the great Raw Materials Division (Kriegsrohstoffabteilung) of the War Office which by the close of the war was larger than all the rest of the War Office put together. It gathered in from private owners all the metal that could be spared for the use of the army. Its subsidiaries were at work seizing the spoil of conquered territory for the same uses, the justification for which in German eyes lay in the fact that the citizens of Germany were equally subject to government exaction. Alongside it, science worked at the creative task of finding substitutes for supplies that were lacking, or new sources of energy for both destruction and recovery.

This organization of war industry which centered in Rathenau's office in the War Ministry was, of course, only a section of the readjustment of the German economic system for purposes of war. No walk of life was left untouched by the disturbing and imperious demands of war economy. The achievement was one of which Germany has every reason to be proud; but it was also one which misled even the most competent observers by creating a false impression of complete success. The depletion of the available stocks of goods at the opening of the war seemed to be only a comparatively minor aspect of the depletion of wealth, for under the stimulus of war-time organization their replacement or even their increase proved to be a far easier task than economists had reckoned with. The result was that by the time this process had gone on for a couple of years economists, as in the case of Professor Cassell, were maintaining that the adaptability of modern industry to the processes of war and its productive capacity were such that the economic power of resistance remained unimpaired by the depletion of stocks, for its increased productive capacity could take care of the increased demand. This point of view was widely shared as the miracle of wartime endurance in all the warring countries seemed to have overthrown all previous conceptions of the laws of economics. It was only later that it was possible to see how greatly the productive capacity had been overtaxed for non-economic ends and how it had been kept going without returns for its maintenance or replacement.

The way in which the increasing strain of war needs weakened both the human and the material resources of industry was not fully evident as long as there was a continuing hope in Germany of a war of conquest in which the victims would ultimately repay Germany for its gigantic effort to impose its will upon Europe and the world. Already in 1915 there were disquieting signs of difficulties in the heavy industries, such as the reduction of coal to 77 per cent of the pre-war output and pig iron to 59 per cent; but this was not permitted to interfere with the production of the materials necessary for the War, and the greatest monthly output of steel during the War was in May 1917. The iron ore that had formerly come from Spain, Morocco or Russia was largely supplied by the exploitation of the ore in French Lorraine and later in Belgium, as well as by the further development of domestic deposits. Manganese ore mining was increased both within Germany and Hungary, and in the Balkans and Asia Minor. The copper mines of Serbia and Poland gave increased supplies, and while the domestic petroleum production remained insignificant in spite of doubled output, the Rumanian oil wells destroyed during the evacuation were restored and put into operation under German engineers. The output of the food and feed crops, contrary to the development in the basic industries, began to decline in acute proportions as early as 1916, and from then on the privations of the German people through food shortage developed into actual distress. Yet, by an immense effort, the impoverished soil was made to bring forth all it was possible for it to produce; more lands were put under the plow on heaths and moorlands; gardens were made on abandoned lands around towns and cities; "war bread" with potato meal was obligatory, and food strictly rationed. Thus a minimum of subsistence was assured for the four years.

War-time need, however, took tribute of German science as it set about the conquest of nature to supply substitutes for those things which were most necessary. The word *Ersatz* became an almost universal word, as the rest of the world observed with admiration and sought to copy the methods employed to secure substitutes for essential things no longer available. *Ersatzwirtschaft*, or the economy of substitutes, spread over the whole field of science. Experiments were made on all kinds of war materials, clothing and goods. In all this, Germany was mobilizing intelligence both for its defense and its endurance.

The most outstanding accomplishment in this field was the establishment of two great plants for the fixation of nitrogen in the production of synthetic ammonia. Here was something that was destined to be of value when the war was over, when the output would be used only as fertilizer and not for high explosives. There is perhaps no greater romance in the history of applied science than that of Leunewerke, the great fixation plant in the heart of Saxony. In 1917, sugar-beet fields gave place to square miles of furnaces, vats and tubing to tap the illimitable air above and "fix" its nitrogen for war or commerce.

Equally dramatic were the developments of chemistry in the use of coal and its derivatives. There is a city, Leverkusen, on the Rhine, which is wholly a creation of coal tar and its derivatives, from lubricants to chemicals and aniline dyes. It was here that poison gas was developed for the war by chemists working side by side with others who never ceased throughout those years to try to discover the remedy for sleeping sickness. A striking example of the universal reach of modern science!

The development of cellulose was fully as important, although perhaps less spectacular. It became a substitute for cotton in the manufacture of explosives. It was distilled for the production of alcohol, both for general industrial uses and as motor fuel. Alcohol was also produced through the distillation of calcium carbide; sulphur was obtained from gypsum, and synthetic camphor from turpentine oil. For clothing and food, science used wood for "artificial wool" and nettles and other weeds for yarn.

In proportion as a nation devotes its efforts to the purposes of war, it lessens them correspondingly or at least to a very considerable degree in other respects. There is, to be sure, a considerable amount of new-found energy in the stimulus of war time; many people are then at work who in time of peace are consumers and not producers of the nation's wealth. But war economics discriminates against many of the things that people find most worth while under normal conditions and against those ways of living which do not contribute to national strength. This means that war economics, even while expending increased energy, leaves undone many things that make life more worth living. The "non-essential" industries are curtailed, with the result that there is a great displacement of both labor and capital. Housing, for example, fell in 1916 to one-ninth of the pre-war amount and in 1917 to one-twelfth, thus leaving a vastly increased demand when the war was over. Municipal services, public utilities and the building and maintenance of roads were much curtailed. Even the railroads, necessary as they were for the movement of troops, were discriminated against in the steel industry, the supply of steel rails diminishing sixty per cent between 1913 and 1917; on the other hand the munition works forged ahead at prodigious speed.

It is surprising to see how far the pressure of war needs lessened efficiency in even the most necessary industries. For example, in spite of the vital problem of food supply, agricultural machinery, once one of the glories of German industry, almost ceased to be produced and the machinery plants when not converted to war uses were shut down. This, at a time when there was a growing shortage of draught animals, reflected the dramatic dilemma which Germany faced during the war, that of having to choose between "food or fodder," that is, the immediate use of the fields for human food or the reconversion of them into food for animals. This gave rise to a violent controversy which went on through the war years and continued afterwards between the advocates of the immediate interests of consumers, mostly city dwellers, and those of the more permanent interests of agricultural production. Shortage of labor and of fertilizers caused a tendency to turn from high-yield, intensive crops, such as sugar beets and potatoes, toward lower yield where less work was involved, such as grain and forage crops. It was in this connection that so much reclamation work was done on heath and moor-

lands, an effort, however, which did not compensate for
the loss of livestock or exhaustion of the soil through lack
of fertilizer and the depletion of farming equipment.

This stimulus to production called for a similar effort
in distribution; for the goods had to get to the consumer.
Although the motor truck was much in use for the haul-
age of military supplies, there was no such great network
of country roads or trunk lines from city to city as are to
be found in Germany today; and the railway played so
great a part in transporting both supplies and armies from
East to West and back again, that the war was sometimes
termed in Germany "the railway war" (*Eisenbahnkrieg*).
Yet, in spite of the superb management of the military
control of the railroads, as early as 1916 they proved
utterly unable to serve adequately both the requirements
of war industry and the food supply of the cities. This
situation was never remedied, because the final effort
launched under the "Hindenburg Program" called for
still further discrimination in the allotment of resources
and increased the strain on the railways. One might have
expected that under these circumstances the railway services would have been included among those essential for
the prosecution of the war, but that was not done; probably out of pure convention, with no economic or technical
justification. The result was that as regards the supply
of labor, the railways were denied the benefit of the
National Service Law, and were left to depend largely
upon a substitute personnel, women, aged workers and
disabled soldiers. The railway workers were not granted
the preference in regard to food supply which went to
those in the essential industries. As a result of under-
nourishment, combined with the use of *Ersatz* labor, the
efficiency of the personnel was reduced some thirty or

forty per cent by the end of the war, as compared with 1913. By 1916 freight traffic was much restricted. The discrimination which at first had meant merely giving preference to shipments of war supplies was extended to a system of priorities which led to confusion and a veritable scramble for favors. By the close of the war the German railways were no longer well equipped to serve the direct requirements of the military occupation, while the supply of civilian needs was absolutely inadequate. When one recalls that the German railway system was one of the most perfectly organized and highly staffed systems in the world, one sees how far-reaching was the disorganization of Germany's war-time economy.

The further we proceed with this description of Germany's war-time economics, the more evident it becomes that the military leaders of Germany, along with those of the rest of Europe, had not planned for the kind of thing that war becomes when great nations mobilize the resources of modern science. What had not been foreseen had therefore to be provided for under increasingly adverse circumstances. With complete loyalty, solidarity and steadiness of purpose, Germany girded itself to meet the unforeseen demands upon its strength and its resources. There is a measure of this loyalty, over and above the sacrifices in the field or the effort on the home front, in the way in which the nation responded to the appeals for war loans. There were in all nine war loans floated from September 1914 to September 1918, and the total amount subscribed was over ninety-eight billion marks, exceeding by about a third the amount of British war loans and even surpassing the war loans of the United States. About sixty-four per cent of Germany's war debt was in the form of long-term domestic bonds.

Over against this fact, however, it should be kept in mind that the burden of war-time taxation was relatively less in Germany than was the case with the enemy governments. The constitution of the German Empire had made no provision for such extraordinary taxes as would have to be levied if even an appreciable fraction of war cost were to be paid during the war years. It may be recalled that it was on this question of a military budget that Bismarck in 1862 won his victory over the Prussian Diet for a policy of blood and iron, but the military budget, the control of which he secured on that occasion, was an insignificant fraction of the expenditures demanded on any one front of the World War. The taxation system of the Reich had been so arranged as to throw a heavy burden of domestic government upon the states and municipalities and to direct any discontent that might arise upon the local authorities and thus relieve the structure of the Empire from financial strain. The result, however, was that the Imperial Government was not so free to tax as in the case of highly centralized governments, and make-shift policies in both direct and indirect taxation were devised, all of which were inadequate.

The result of throwing so much of the war finances into the form of loans made the German people conscious partners in the industry of war. At first the confidence of victory maintained the national credit, based on the old military tradition — a tradition as old as history — that the victors could collect from the vanquished. This attitude of mind must not be judged upon the basis of the post-war experience. Except for a few skeptics — among whom Norman Angell was an outstanding figure — people generally believed in 1914 that a victorious war could be profitable. In the years of its defeat, Germany has forgotten how widely this idea was shared when the German armies still seemed capable of imposing their will upon the enemy. The full-hearted way in which this belief found expression in the treaties of Bucharest and Brest-Litovsk is an historical fact which cannot be denied any more than the exactions of the Treaty of Versailles. It is only recently that we have had a full analysis of the negotiations which closed the war on the eastern front, showing what war economics means when the economists are victorious soldiers dealing with a beaten enemy.[4] Friends of Germany always feel that it is unfair to point to the treaties of Brest-Litovsk or Bucharest as indicating what Germany might have done had it been victorious on the western front as well; but without going into that field of conjecture, the fact remains that among the German critics of the Versailles Treaty there were those whose mind and conscience could not have been wholly clear as they pointed to the exactions of the Allies. The German theory of war was as relentless in its treatment of the conquered as it was in the method of government which it employed in the occupied territories. These are facts of history and not conjecture.

A word finally about the occupied territories themselves. At first, and naturally, great hopes were built upon the resources of Belgium and northern France on the west, as well as upon the conquered territories in the east and south. But in every case, except perhaps in parts of Poland and in Serbia — where the Austrians in occupation did surprisingly well — the returns proved far less than had been expected. At first the raw materials and the industrial plants seized in these territories were hailed as

[4] J. W. Wheeler-Bennett, *The Forgotten Peace* (1939).
See also the story of the negotiations at Brest-Litovsk in Gratz and Schüller, *The Economic Policy of Austria-Hungary* (Carnegie Endowment Series).

bringing a much-needed increase to Germany's military strength. But so far as war industries were concerned, this was only the case so long as the spoils of war were readily accessible. When the existing supplies were used up in the process of spoliation, replacement was more difficult than at home because man power was either lacking or difficult to manage; and when factories had been robbed of their machines to supply German industries, the problem of unemployment became serious and costly. The effort to transplant workers from Belgium to Germany was a disastrous failure. By fines and financial exactions banks and municipalities were forced to contribute enormous sums; at the opening of 1918, nine months before the end of the war, the Germans themselves estimated that they had taken two hundred million gold francs from the banks of the industrial area of Northern France, while the city of Lille alone paid in fines nearly two hundred million more. But the civilian German administrators were constantly struggling against the demands of the military because they realized what dragons' teeth were being sown for a harvest of hatred and non-co-operation on the part of the sufferers. Allied public opinion has never done justice to the efforts of these non-military administrators of the occupied territories; it would still be a surprise to many of those who remember the name of von Bissing, the Governor General of Belgium, to learn that his chief difficulties were with the generals of his own army.

All in all, the exploitation of the conquered territories proved how little the economy of war can save out of its own destruction for purposes of recovery. Yet it is doubtful if any army in occupation could have set about the task of making war pay with more intelligence and competence than the German War Office employed in attempting to realize upon the resources of Northern France. Fortunately for history, the French, on re-entering the occupied territory, found the manual which was prepared under the German General Staff for the purposes of German industry by some two hundred technical experts, describing in detail and assessing the value of every particle of industrial property in over four thousand establishments in the area behind the lines. It mapped out even the cottages where the women made the lace of Valenciennes as well as the mines and factories along the border of Belgium. Everything was accounted for so that the Organization for Raw Materials and Machines which had developed out of Rathenau's original effort at economic mobilization should be able to profit best from the spoil of the conquered. The document has been reprinted and is available in our libraries. Its authenticity has been acknowledged by the German government itself, which justifies it on the basis of a retaliation against England's blockade and also on the ground that the conquered territory should be considered as an integral part of that of the conqueror. If German citizens were obliged to surrender every useful article for war purposes down to door knobs and bedsteads, why should the citizens of enemy countries be spared? But the argument thus set forth in a document for the use of the German Delegation at the Paris Peace Conference would hardly have convinced the former owners of the industrial plants of northern France whose factories had been dismantled, their doors swinging loosely in the wind and weeds growing high across their entrances.

Most of the detail of this story has been told in the various volumes of *The Economic and Social History of the World War* referred to below.[5] But no economist in Ger-

[5] See Chapter VIII.

many has gone to the heart of the matter and shown the cost to the victor of the process of spoliation. For one thing it was a process obscured by the fact that during the war there was a succession of conquests, so that each one offered its spoils in the initial stages of exploitation, and when the returns began to lessen from that source new sources were sought elsewhere or new devices applied in the territories already overrun. Necessary as were the goods received at the time, the displacements caused by reliance upon such temporary contributions left the situation fundamentally unsound. This is, of course, but another way of stating the obvious fact that the emergency nature of wartime economics calls for activities that are fundamentally hostile to long-term prosperity.

CHAPTER III

FROM THE HINDENBURG PROGRAM
TO INFLATION

OF all the revolutions in history none has been more complete within its field than the revolution in warfare with which this study deals, when the era of hand industry was superseded by that of mass production. Although some appreciation of the magnitude of the change in military operations due to the advent of science was already shown in the pre-war preparations and there had been increasing awareness of it as the World War wore on through 1915, it was not until 1916 that the full consequences of what had happened were borne in upon the warring governments. That was the year of Verdun and the Somme, perhaps the most tragic year for Western Europe in all history. By December, both sides were counting the cost and reshaping their plans for the final stage of the conflict, which still eluded them. In Great Britain, Lloyd George displaced Asquith from the Premiership and a vigorous War Cabinet undertook to mobilize the nation at home for increased strength in the field. In France, Briand also reconstituted his cabinet, bringing three dynamic figures to the fore, Albert Thomas and Loucheur as Minister and Undersecretary of Munitions with Herriot in charge of Supplies. Germany did not wait for their example. Already on December 2, the Reichstag, by 235 votes against 19, had passed its National Service Law for the control and mobilization of the whole strength of the nation for war. This called for the forced labor of the German people for two main purposes: to repair the wastage in men and materials after the terrible expenditure of both in the great battles on the Western Front and the continued drain in the East; and to repair the shortage in domestic supplies, both in the necessities of life and in credit or money. The plan was grandiose in outline, a living embodiment of national solidarity and therefore a buttress to morale. While the army authorities were combing out men from every walk in life who were still fit for military service, industrialists were supplied with substitutes in factories and mills. The crux of the situation lay in coal and iron, the supply of which had seemed inexhaustible when Rathenau's plan was begun in 1914; but the law covered everything.

This national plan bore the misleading but effective title of "The Hindenburg Program." The old Marshal, however, supplied only his name — the one name to conjure with in Germany at the time. The chief architect was Dr. Helfferich, the Vice Chancellor, but behind it lay the pioneering work begun in August 1914 by Dr. Walter Rathenau. Dr. Helfferich represented the interests of finance, industry and shipping, having the confidence of its more conservative leaders. His successor in this regard was Hugenberg, Hitler's powerful supporter. At the War Office, General Groener and Colonel Koeth, competent specialists, were helpful, the former doubly so because the trade unionists had confidence in his democratic convictions. They knew that they were already on the defensive, because it became clear that the Prussian War Ministry was set upon using the plan to prevent criticism of the costly failure at Verdun or any signs of that disaffection which they had begun to suspect among the working class. This was the beginning of that legend referred to above, of "the dagger thrust in the back" of which the reactionaries falsely accused the Socialists, and which the Nazis have made into an article of faith. How false and slanderous this charge has been is evidenced by the fact that during the two years of the operation of the National Service Law, the Government accepted the proposals of the Trade Union leaders in almost every case and carried them out. The coöperation of labor was as loyal as it professed to be in the following resolution which was unanimously passed at a great meeting of 500 delegates held a few days after the law was enacted:

The representatives of some four million organized workmen and employees assembled in Germania Hall on December 12 declare their readiness to coöperate with all their forces in carrying out the National Service Law.

The classes represented in the organization of workmen and employees are willing to put their whole strength, as a complete unit, at the service of the country, in order that the plans of our adversaries for the destruction of Germany may fail.

The assembled representatives expect that the Imperial Government and the War Office will give far-reaching encouragement to the legitimate demands of workmen and employees in the matter of better conditions of labor, higher wages, and guaranties for the maintenance of free association (*Koalitionsrecht*). We also demand stronger measures against profiteering in food and other necessities of life and a fairer distribution of existing supplies, so that the working population can fulfil the demands made upon them.

The attitude of the leaders of German trade unionism toward the National Service Law is reflected in the follow-

ing statement by one of the soundest leaders of German
trade unionism, Paul Umbreit.[1] The passage is worth quot-
ing in full because it shows how well satisfied upon the
whole the trade unions were with the way in which this
mobilization of wartime industry dealt with labor.

The National Service Law certainly did much, during the
period of nearly two years in which it remained in force, to
heighten the volume of war production. Its immediate consequence, however, was the decline of German industry and,
in the case of raw materials, a complete impoverishment of
Germany's economic system. Anything and everything that
seemed of any possible use for war purposes — factories,
machinery, laboratories and every kind of institution — was
forced into the compass of this, the last mobilization of all
available forces, and was used up in it. The downfall of our
fatherland, in the long run, was not halted by this procedure;
it was made complete and universal. National Service completely exhausted the forces of resistance which lived in our
people, and in the end led to Germany's unconditional surrender to the conditions of peace imposed by the enemy. As a
measure of strategy or a political device the Hindenburg
Program failed, because it overstrained the forces of the nation.
As a measure of social policy and of national economy the
National Service Law, on the contrary, was a success; and the
working-class, more than any other, had reason to be satisfied
with it, thanks to the form it had taken in Parliament through
the coöperation of the trade-unions with the political parties.
The guaranties which had been introduced in the interest of
the employed as a corollary to compulsory service were so
satisfactory that there was never a labor revolt against the
National Service Law. Neither were trade-unionist organizations in any way oppressed by it; on the contrary, their posi-

[1] *Der Krieg und die Arbeitsverhältnisse*, p. 262. (Carnegie Endowment Series.)

tion was strengthened and they won great numbers of new adherents through the amplification of war industry. With the end of the War came the abrogation of the National Service Law, by decree of the Council of People's Commissaries, on November 11, 1918. The works committees, however, and the conciliation boards remained, and the provisions of the law in regard to them have been reënacted in the laws of the Republic.

Evidently it was not Labor which failed the Fatherland under the Hindenburg Program, but the Program itself. This at least was the judgment of the Minister of Finance, Dr. Schiffer, in 1919, as he summed up the situation as follows from the point of view of German capital in the debates of the Weimar Assembly.

I don't want to criticize the Hindenburg Program from the military point of view. Economically it was a program of despair and did an enormous amount of damage. A reaction of the most disgusting character set in. Expense was no longer taken into consideration. It was as if a premium had been put on luring away the workmen from one industry to another offering higher wages, or to a position more secure from enlistment in the army. In the place of organization, disorder reigned, without any fixed relation to reality. In fact, the system from which we suffer today began to develop. The material and moral damage done was absolutely terrific.

It goes without saying that this point of view is not shared by those who put the blame for Germany's ills upon the peace treaty and the post-war policy of the allies rather than upon the damage caused by war economy. For example, Professor Lotz,[2] although freely admitting the

[2] *Die deutsche Staatsverwaltung im Weltkriege*, p. 108. (Carnegie Endowment Series.)

damage done to the normal peace-time economy of Germany by the impact of the war upon it as registered in the Hindenburg Program, nevertheless holds to the view that had it not been for the peace treaty and the post-war policy of the allies, that damage would not have been beyond repair. How wrong this judgment is, although it became the orthodoxy of German opinion under the propaganda directed against the Treaty, can be seen by a study of the statistics of Dr. Grebler. But the real effects of such disturbances are registered less in the statistics of national accounting than in the social history of the people concerned. It is now clear that the Hindenburg Program — which, we must continually remind ourselves, was war economy at work — was the first step which Germany took on the path toward National Socialism. That this was the case has been pointed out by competent historians, but the full import of it has apparently not yet been realized either inside or outside of Germany. Nazi Germanism fed upon the discontent which was concentrated upon the Treaty of Versailles, but its origins lay in the wartime mobilization of Germany's strength for war purposes in 1917.

The whole situation was admirably summed up by Albrecht Mendelssohn Bartholdy, the former Director of the Institute for Foreign Policy at Hamburg. Although a victim of the blind fury of anti-Semite persecution, this grandson of the great musician maintained to the last that nobility of mind, which had long done honor to German science. In his posthumous work, "*The War and German Society*," [3] written as a testament of a liberal, he sums up the total effect upon German society of the Hindenburg Program in the following terms.

[3] In the Carnegie Endowment Series.

Nothing was farther from the minds of those with whom the Hindenburg Program originated than to strengthen the position of the Socialist party. But that was the only tangible effect it finally had. Through its disregard of every sound relation between work and wages it helped to create conditions which, even apart from the effects of inflation, would have made the return to a normal state of things in industry and labor almost impossible. The severity of the reaction against the power secured by trade-unionist organizations under the National Service Law was one of the most conspicuous features of the political revulsion in Germany. It is one of the personal tragedies of this time that the second President of the Republic, in order to undo some of the consequences of the war program connected with his name, felt compelled to sign the emergency decree by which the National Socialist Party was put into power, their program being to restore the German nation to the condition in which it fought the war from 1915 to 1917.

The monetary disturbances which came to their climax in the inflation of 1923–1924 cannot be traced to a single source nor can the Hindenburg Program be said to have been one of their primary causes. We should be nearer the truth if we likened its influence on German currency to that of an abnormally narrow gorge through which the waters of public finance had to take their course, accelerating their pace as the gorge became deeper and deeper. The primary causes were doctrinarianism, as it manifested itself in the financial mobilization plans and the inherent weakness of the policy of the Government – if it can be called a policy – in trying to finance the War mainly through an anticipation of a speedy and decisive victory. Public credit lasted through the first two years of the War, digesting the internal loans which were to cover the bill of military and political expenses for the next six months or so. It did better, on the whole, than could have been expected. Its chief mainstay, during that period, was the profound belief of the people, and especially those with small savings and a moderate income, in the War as their common destiny. If they were taking refuge in war as a means of national policy somebody might certainly have had enough common sense and enough cynicism, too, to say: If we are planning wars let us train ourselves in preparedness for them. Let us distribute the task among all in the most rational way and conduct the war, once it has been launched, in a way which will mean a minimum of loss and a maximum of gain. To do that, our financial policy must be one of calculating the cost, spreading the risk over a long period, and involving as many other countries as possible in the system of war credits we shall need to carry the war through if a military success is not given to us by pitched battles.

But as this was not a planned or an intended war — though it had often been rehearsed on the green cloth of ministerial war offices — everybody believed in the necessity of carrying its burden as his ordained fate, and the heavier the better. To the common people who subscribed to loans to the best of their power great strength of endurance grew out of such a conviction. To the Government it was the reverse — a dispensing with solid, sober reasoning and with that sense of stern responsibility which should have rested on the heads of officialdom even during the reign of war. The amount of short-term treasury bonds, which meant the debt owed by the Reich to the Reichsbank (or in other words the amount which had to be raised through the next internal loan if the Reich was to be able to redeem the bonds when due) had risen from 897 million marks in October, 1914, to 3,412 millions in October, 1915, to 7,856 in October, 1916, and to 22,679 millions in October, 1917. It was doubled again during the next year, and almost doubled from 1918 to 1919. But 1916 to 1917 showed the maximum rate of increase.

That is one side of the question. The other is that taxation during the War went quite as unmistakably wrong as did credit policy. It was not only that war profits were allowed to escape taxation during the War to a remarkable degree — especially if

Germany in the War be compared to Great Britain. Taxation, where it really reached out and made a financial success of a special surtax, as it did in the cases of the additional taxes on coal and on cigarettes, defeated its own ends by fastening on just the kind of object which had to be purchased in enormous quantities by the administration itself. The tax was laid upon the buyer, and the principal buyer who paid anything that was asked for was the Government, which had tried to raise money through taxation. That is where the Hindenburg Program came in and, causing expenses to rise to a sum irretrievable, through internal loans, let it become a patent truth that at the end of the War — whenever it did come — there would exist a public debt that could not be repaid to the creditors, if it could be paid at all, without serious danger to the currency and to capitalism in general.

Inflation, arising from a plan for financial mobilization which proceeded on lines of strictly capitalistic reasoning, and Dictatorship, arising from a program for national service which seemed to stabilize the trade unions in their dominant political position — that is what follows when war takes a hand in the game.

From this hurried sketch of German war economy it is easy to see how confusing it was bound to be to those living under it and how this confusion was not likely to be dissipated readily in the post-war years if a wholly new explanation of Germany's ills were injected into the problem of recovery. There had been nothing in history parallel to this siege of half Europe by the Allied blockade, and nothing parallel to the methods by which Germany and Austria sought to meet it. As "the war that couldn't last six weeks" grew into the war that lasted four years and falsified the predictions of economists, the idea of war as an economy of destruction seemed more and more open to question. The inevitable consequences of such a complete subordination of welfare to militant needs seemed not to have been inevitable after all. Apparently modern industrial society was much stronger than had been dreamed of; although weakened, its resiliency was still to be reckoned with. New assets, as we have seen, were opened up to strengthen it; conquered territories, the exploitation of Germany's unused resources and the triumphs of science. These achievements were heralded with almost as much acclaim as victories in the field. They kept the morale of the civilian population up to the heavy task of holding out in what was termed "the home defense" of the fatherland. They helped one to forget the hardships by maintaining the confidence of victory. If that victory had been won, if the unlimited submarine warfare had succeeded, as it would have but for the convoy system, or if Ludendorff's drive for Paris had not been stopped and Germany could have forced the defeated Allies to her terms, the true nature of her war economy would have been still further obscured. No one seems to have been aware of the extent to which the economic structure had been gutted by the world-conflagration. The people of Germany themselves could hardly be blamed for not appreciating this, when the delusion of its capacity for speedy recovery was so strongly held by its ex-enemies that, even after the disastrous peace of Versailles, they invested millions in marks to reap the profits from Germany's industrial plant which could achieve such miracles in war.

Perhaps the best way to see how war economics creates delusions that obscure its real nature is to turn first to that section of it which, in Germany, seemed most to contradict the principles of orthodox economic teaching. This was in the field of science. There the achievements of war-time reached far beyond the striking successes in finding substitutes for materials lacking because of the blockade and became a vast and splendid conquest of nature itself. Chemistry had more than a Roman triumph when organized industry placed at its disposal the strength of legions, not only for use in battle but also on the home front. But great as its developments were, most of them were too costly to be carried on profitably in peace-time. Synthetic rubber was not yet commercially valuable as a substitute for natural rubber. Low-grade ores can be used as substitutes, but only necessity justifies turning to them if high-grade ores are accessible in the world market. Machinery converted for war production, as in the leather and textile industries, involved uneconomical outlays which had to be written off as normal demands succeeded the high-pressure needs of war. Standardization as a means of reducing costs was in line with peace-time developments; but it was forced along uneconomic lines and proved to be an added source of loss in certain instances because of its tendency to check ready adjustment to changing markets in the post-war period of transition. Worse still, as we have seen above, the manufacturing equipment in general had so deteriorated due to rapid wear in war-time that shortage in machinery parts and supplies could not be made up. The dilapidated condition of plants, due to transfers of parts from less to more essential war industries, especially under the Hindenburg Program, called for heavy expenditures. Mines had suffered from "predatory exploitation," especially in the case of coal, where the damage due to war-time haste and waste (Raubbau) is estimated to have left the mines twice as poor as the decreased coal supplies indicated. The failure to replace or improve machinery was especially to be found in those industries which produced consumers' goods, especially textiles. On the other hand, it was not easy suddenly to stop the war-time activities which were too costly for peace. Machine construction, electrical and chemical appliances had grown beyond normal needs and, therefore, much beyond the needs of an exhausted world.

In short, although the war changed and in part improved German industrial machinery, it largely denatured the process at the same time, as the post-war years were to show. Against the wastage and loss must be balanced the creation of new organizations of business to eliminate uneconomical competition. Armed with the new capacity for production great cartels grew greater, confident that they could meet any future — if only the servitudes of the Treaty of Versailles could be removed so as to give them a free field in the world market. Even as it was, such a powerful unit as the German Chemical Trust felt sure of itself. With its unique equipment, which the new rival in the United States could not hope to match, it had no fear that it could not reconquer its place in the world. But one thing it, along with all the rest, failed to appreciate, was that the war itself had so largely destroyed the consumption market. The need was greater than ever; but the buying power less. This left the enlarged plant an excessive investment, which could only be fully employed if the conditions of peace-time operation were as abnormal in their way as those of the war had been. Certainly there would be no place for such an economy if the world market were to return to the relatively narrower confines of pre-war conditions.

To meet this problem, a readjustment of markets was planned in the creation of a great Mitteleuropa, a closed economic preserve covering the two middle European empires and their satellites. This was actually negotiated between Germany and Austria-Hungary during the War. Long-drawn-out bargaining had ended in a document signed at Salzburg on October 11, 1918, just a few weeks before the Armistice made waste paper of the agreement — at least for the next twenty years.[4] The peace treaties prevented any revival of this scheme, so long as they were in effect. The futile effort made by Germany, in 1931, to form a customs union with Austria showed that it was yet too soon to throw off the treaty prohibitions, in view of the political implications of such an economic unity. Before very long, however, in various disguises, Dr. Schacht brought the program into the political arena again, with his barter economy and monopolistic trading. But it played no part in European history during the years when German economy was still linked with war recovery.

Justification for the advocates of Mitteleuropa was offered in the impediments erected by other countries to the entry of German goods. These markets were speedily closed by protective-tariff legislation, especially in the United States. It was wholly natural that American industry should be apprehensive of post-war dumping by friend and foe alike, as they strove to set their economic machinery going again. But few of those who blame the Allies for their failure to pay war debts remember how our tariff policy made payment well-nigh impossible; and fewer still seem to recall the impediment it created to German economic recovery. For good or ill, the world had become one to an extent recognized only in the defensive acts of protective recoil against economic invasion.

There remained another way of escape from the conditions arising out of the war, one that was actually tried — that of inducing foreign capital to take the risk of refinanc-

---

[4] There is a unique account of this in the volume by Gratz and Schüller, *The Economic Policy of Austria-Hungary* (Carnegie Endowment Series).

ing the hard-pressed German economy. It did not need much inducing. In spite of reparations, German credit was still good in the eyes of private investors in foreign lands. How much of their savings went into municipal bonds for such projects as rehousing or enterprises like canal-building or railroad construction, or into business investments, is difficult to calculate. Before this process was over inflation had set in and money ceased almost to be a stable unit of value. But it is generally agreed that, in terms of the investor, Germany borrowed, mainly in the United States, more than double the amount which she paid on account of her reparation obligations.

Even this, however, was not enough. The next step was inflation, to lessen money costs to both government and business. The government was concerned because of unemployment, threatening internal difficulties, the end of which no one could foresee. This, at least, was the excuse for costly new public works, carried on at a time when neither England nor France ventured on similar expenditures to anything like the same degree, with the single and inevitable exception of rebuilding the devastated areas. This evidence of what looked like Government extravagance did not pass unnoticed in France. Its natural effect was to harden the opposition to any lessening of reparation payments. French cities were not having their slums torn down and modern apartment houses built for their working people. The feeling grew that Germany was both more able to meet its reparation obligations than it admitted and that it was following policies intended to lead to default. German good faith was at stake; and in the unfriendly eyes of so close a student of finance as Poincaré, it stood condemned. The occupation of the Ruhr had another and rather trivial immediate excuse in the failure of Germany to deliver the agreed amount of timber and coal, but the real cause lay in the character of German financial policy.

There is no doubt that this policy was open to very serious criticism; but, as we shall see, the problem which it had to face was almost unsolvable. In the earliest days of the Republic, it set about putting its house in order by a series of taxation reforms which go under the name of their sponsor, Erzberger. There were to be national taxes paid in to the government of the Republic to an extent undreamed of in the pre-war Empire, which had little more than customs duties for the normal running of the Government. For the first time, there was to be a Treasury as a department of the Central Government. Its officials were to assess and levy the taxes necessary for the extraordinary demands of that time. In carrying out these purposes, however, it met with obstacles on all sides. The Treasury officials had no such tradition of authority behind them as those in other branches of the Government, and more especially as existed in Prussia and the States; and lacking authority they received little or no coöperation from the great industries which would normally have furnished the chief sources of Government revenue. The result was to leave an undue burden upon indirect taxation which normally fell heavily upon the consuming public, more especially those of limited income, salaried and wage workers. This weakness in the administration of tax collecting was one of the chief causes for that kind of discontent with the Republic which was soon to furnish ammunition to the Nazi agitators. It was believed, and there is good evidence to support the belief, that leaders in industrial organizations and at least some of those in the banking world eluded taxation to a scandalous extent. This also was a point that by no means escaped attention in France and England, where it was felt that the weakness of the German government in its failure to collect the taxes due it was in the nature of a connivance with business, in order to turn over to it rather than to reparation such funds as were actually available. Along with the extravagance in government expenditure, they regarded it as an evidence of bad faith.

Ultimately the chief sufferer from this weakness in fiscal policy was, of course, the German government itself. The choice lay between economy and inflation. It is part of the accepted doctrine that the great inflation of 1922 and 1923, when German money became worth less than the paper it was printed on, was due to the Treaty of Versailles. No one would dream of denying that this was largely true, especially in view of German psychology at the time. But the theory that the treaty was the sole cause will not stand examination, any more than that the sole cause was Germany's own fault in conniving at policies destined to bring it about. That there was some connivance cannot be denied; nor indeed has it been denied by those in a position to know. But that is not to say that the Government of the Republic followed a persistent policy of bad faith. It must be remembered that the solution for unemployment, when it reaches dangerous proportions, has always been government works or some form of subsidy to prevent starvation or sedition. The Republic that had this problem on its hands was not firmly enough in the saddle to deal with the situation as courageously as was the case in England where the government deliberately chose to support finance instead of commerce and industry and so for a number of years at least maintained intact "the empire of sterling." In little Czechoslovakia, the sturdy integrity of Dr. Rasin, the Minister of Finance, achieved the miracle of stabilizing his currency in the very midst of a Europe where money

was running beyond control.[5] But the extent of the bitter-
ness which such policies engendered is to be measured by
the fact that he, along with Erzberger and Rathenau, was
slain by the assassin's bullet. The prime causes of inflation
lay in the continuing disturbances of the War upon the
social as well as the economic structure of German life and
the apparent inability of the Government to deal effectively
with such vast and pressing problems. Whether the exactions of the Treaty made the solution of these problems
economically impossible, as is generally believed, or
whether Germany could have met them as it offered to do
at Paris, is a matter for pure speculation. The whole issue
passed from economics to politics when Poincaré went into
the Ruhr.

[5] See the volume by A. Rasin, *The Financial Policy of Czechoslovakia
During the First Year of Its History* (Carnegie Endowment Series).

CHAPTER IV

THE FALSE RECOVERY

IN 1923 Germany plumbed the depth of national despair. The French occupation of the Ruhr was more than an effort to collect from a defaulting debtor; the German people regarded it as a blow at the industrial heart of a nation which had come to live by industry. In the Ruhr itself both owners and workers were given the hard choice of keeping the mills and mines going under the occupation of alien troops, or letting engineering machinery be ruined by stoppage. In the rest of Germany there was a sense of utter defeat and helplessness. The resentment against the French was bitter to the point of sullen wrath which had all the elements of war psychology. The presence of black troops in French garrisons in occupied Germany added fuel to the resentment. Indeed, it is doubtful if, in the heart of the war, there was ever such a wave of hatred as that invoked by the policy of Poincaré. It strengthened the tendency to believe everything bad about the Allied and Associated Powers, England's "duplicity" and Wilson's "betrayal" of the fourteen points.

Then, in the midst of these national humiliations, came the utter destruction of the German mark, the symbol of its economic strength and its business integrity. It was but natural that this last and greatest catastrophe should be

thought of as wholly arising from the others, that the Inflation was caused by the exactions of the Treaty of Versailles; and this belief has been widely shared in other
countries as well. We have already seen that this conclusion is not true, if by it is meant that the German Government was a passive victim of its ex-enemy neighbors,
and that all the blame should fall upon their shoulders. The
failure to put its own house in order was a major factor in
starting the great Inflation on its devastating course. The
need for fiscal reform in the Reich was recognized by all
thoughtful Germans; yet the discussions of numerous commissions and sub-commissions failed to produce any adequate remedy. Labor objected to bearing the burden of
indirect taxes which struck at consumers; industry argued
that a heavy increase in direct taxation would prevent the
expansion and strengthening of the chief instrument in the
recovery of Germany as a whole; while the landed pro-
prietors were especially unyielding in their opposition to
proposals which would make the tax yield increase in proportion to the depreciation of the mark.

However valid these reasons may have seemed from the
political point of view, the fact remains that Germany did
not tax itself as heavily to meet the bills which were falling
due as was the case in England, France and the United
States. Some idea of the relative burden of taxation in 1923
may be gained from a comparative statement issued by
Chancellor Snowden of the British Exchequer on February
28, 1924. In issuing it he pointed out that "international
comparisons of this nature require to be used with great
caution" because of the differing financial systems of the
various countries. Nevertheless, the discrepancy shown by
the following table is so great as to indicate very clearly
the unsolved problem of post-war Germany.

	National Tax Burden Per Head				
	1913 or 1913–14 (Actual) In Sterling at par			In 1923 or 1923–24 (Estimated) In Sterling at par	
United Kingdom..........	3	11	0	15	18	0
France	3	7	0	6	18	2
United States (Federal)	1	7	11	6	14	10
Germany (Reich)	1	10	8	4	1	4
Italy	2	2	8	3	6	11
Canada (Dominion)	3	8	2	7	19	8
Australia (Commonwealth) .	3	8	1	8	1	9
South Africa (Union)	1	9	0	3	9	11
New Zealand	6	3	0	12	5	3

It will be seen from this table that the estimated tax burden per head in Germany in 1923–24 was only a little more than one-fourth of what the English were paying.

The disastrous consequence of this fiscal policy was shown up fully when the French were in the Ruhr. Passive resistance was financed by printing notes with the consequence that inflation which had been slowly rising became a vast and devastating tide.

It is hard to describe what happened in Germany during the Inflation because money became meaningless and the cost of living changed not only from week to week but from day to day and from hour to hour. When money loses its value, people try at once to get rid of it for goods that may at least have some kind of use or may be bartered later for other goods. I recall a scene on a Friday afternoon when the week's work was over in a great industrial plant. At the sounding of the whistle, a mob of running workers raced to the factory store with their week's wages and in an hour's time the shelves were empty. Boots and shoes, and clothes and groceries had all been seized for hoarding or use by those who knew that by the next morning their money would have gone down to a fraction of its value. It was scenes like these that burned themselves into the memory of the German people more than the fact that the American dollar became for a while the standard by which the mark was measured in Berlin. Some idea of the scale of this measurement may be gained from the fact that on July 3, 1923, one dollar was worth 160,000 paper marks on the Berlin Bourse. By November 20th in that year, when the Inflation came to its conclusion, the value of the mark was "stabilized" at the rate of 4,200 billion marks for a dollar.[1]

Then came "the miracle of the mark." The worthless paper money gave way to the so-called Rentenmark, a new currency behind which stood the guarantee of the wealth of Germany. The Rentenmark was, according to all the orthodox treatises on banking, based on the poorest kind of security, a lien or national mortgage of real property and national establishments. But no one thought of calling for the property which it represented; by common consent the German people treated the money as real in itself, while the Government was cautious enough not to strain this confidence by too rapid a flotation of the money. In any case, the recovery of confidence saved the country from the incredible situation in which so much of the savings of the German people had been swallowed up. Then, with the Dawes Plan giving definite limits to reparation in 1924, another "miracle" happened: that of the balanced budget of 1925. Both at home and abroad these signs of German economic stability were

---

[1] For a detailed analysis and masterly criticism of the treatment of this question, see *The Economics of Inflation, A Study of Currency Depreciation in Post-War Germany*, by Costantino Bresciani-Turroni (London, 1937). Professor Bresciani-Turroni was a member of the staff of the Reparations Commission, then head of the Export Control and economic adviser to the Agent-General for Reparation.

hailed almost unanimously as the beginning of a final recovery of German economy as a whole from the effect of the World War. This interpretation of the German achievement seemed proven by the growing prosperity which, according to statements at the time, by 1928 had increased the income of the average German, in real terms, 15½ per cent higher than in 1913.[2] If the history of the world had only stopped then, there would be no way of disproving this culmination of the series of economic miracles which began in Germany's war-time achievements. But for that matter the same miraculous story might have been written about almost the whole of the civilized world; for the gains made in Germany were, as Professor Angell pointed out, in line with the general European advance and far less than those in the United States.[3] It was the age of hope and of illusion. When Professor Angell's book was written fortunes were literally being made over night in Wall Street and other money markets, as the whole world speculated in the possibility of securing title deeds to the creative energy and unlimited resources of a new industrial revolution much greater than that of a century ago. What the holders of these stocks and bonds forgot was that the World War had not only set every person borrowing upon his future but had brought about a lessening of markets for the finished goods

[2] James W. Angell, *The Recovery of Germany*, p. 320.
[3] In an article in the *New York Times Magazine* of December 3, 1939, Mr. Geoffrey Crowther, Editor of *The Economist*, relies on this analysis of Professor Angell published on the very eve of the catastrophic crash of 1929, to prove that the War, once it was over, brought little or no perceptible impoverishment to the three main European participants. Mr. Crowther is surprised that any one doubts this conclusion "since there is so little evidence" to support the contrary! The article is a good index of the way in which economists of high standing have pronounced *ex cathedra* on war economics without bothering to follow the intricate pattern of the problem through in detail.

through the imposition of all kinds of barriers to trade. It is hardly too much to say that the one free thing in the international economic world was the movement of loans and debts.

The Wall Street crash of 1929 proved to be not just the opening of a regular cyclic depression but the beginning of a long period of liquidation, delayed by the false recovery from the War and hampering post-war policies. For a while Europe, including Germany, seemed to be withstanding the pressure of this great blow upon credit with astonishing stability, considering the extent of the crash. But the day of reckoning was only held off for a year and a half; then in the early summer of 1931 the failure of the Credit-Anstalt in Vienna cracked the structure of credit, and a "run" on Germany began, similar to a run on a bank.[4] The weakness of Germany's whole economic position then became evident, depending as it did upon short-term borrowing. For a while it looked as though the German people would have to undergo again the awful experience of the national bankruptcy of 1923. Mindful of the interests of American investors, President Hoover launched his proposal for a moratorium to give the Reich a chance to meet its obligations. To save the day, the statesmen of the leading countries conferred together personally both in European capitals and in Washington, and a "standstill agreement" was agreed to by Germany's creditors. But this proved insufficient to stabilize the finances of a world that had piled a speculative delirium on the top of a devastating war. Although war debts and reparations were thrown into discard — except as political hindrances to the furtherance of good understand-

---

[4] The phrase is from Sir Arthur Salter's *Recovery, the Second Effort,* pp. 49 ff.

ing — in the anxious months which followed, London registered increasing fear of being forced off gold. In September
1931 this finally happened. The thinness of the façade of
Germany's "prosperity" was now sufficiently apparent.
The mark was ultimately saved by practically withdraw-
ing it from international circulation and substituting barter
instead. The brilliant legerdemain of Dr. Schacht postponed again the consequences of this long series of maladjustments arising from the War. The German people
sought their salvation by denying the fundamental laws
of economics, going back far beyond the days of Adam
Smith to the seventeenth century methods of securing in
international marketing a balance in gold, treasure or raw
materials, in order to keep Germany's hard-pressed industry alive. But the ultimate consequences of this have
been the ruin of free industry in Germany and a manipu-
lated trade with the outside world, bringing the threat of
economic reprisals. The outbreak of war in 1939 found
Germany long engaged in economic war.

The fact that in these post-war years problems of currency and banking have been so much more in the public
mind than those of trade and commerce is not without
significance in itself. The world of credit is a world of
debt, — for that is what credit means, — and those who
draw incomes from that debt are, naturally, concerned that
the symbols of their partnership in it should remain unimpaired; for by means of it they hope to make sure that
the goods and services of the future will be theirs when
they need them. The "flight" of the mark, the franc,
the pound and the dollar was therefore catastrophic in the
eyes of all propertied people and the stabilization of currency a first concern not only for the security of financial
investment but also as a necessary basis for industry and

commerce. Now, it was primarily in this field of finance, that is to say of the inter-relation of economic interests, that the World War caused its chief displacement, far more than in the actual destruction of goods. It is, however, much more difficult to trace the workings of credit than the actual movements of commerce or industry, and this difficulty is increased by the fact that they are both parts of one interlocked economy. A good example of this interplay of finance and commerce lies in Germany's own war-time history. Its international credit position was so severely impaired as a result of the War that it had practically to start all over again. Of a total of between 20 and 30 billion gold marks of its pre-war investments abroad, 3 billions had been disposed of during the War, an additional billion of German securities sold abroad, short-term foreign credits between 3 and 4 billion marks had been acquired and, finally, foreign credits in open accounts and paper marks exported abroad, totalling between 6 and 7 billions.[5] To this extent at least was Germany crippled by the War in the financing of its business abroad. An even greater handicap, however, was the high physical cost of production, as old plants were written off and new equipment installed, while the standard of living of the workers had to be maintained. Nevertheless, Germany went ahead to restore its industrial life with the same kind of steady purpose as England put into the recovery of her position as the world's banker.

No precise measurement is possible of the costs of Germany's effort.[6] The early phase can be obscurely fol-

[5] Germany, Statistisches Reichsamt. *Germany's Economic and Financial Condition*. Berlin, 1923, p. 22.

[6] The purely mechanical method of evaluating real costs through the conversion of monetary costs at current prices into gold marks with the aid of price indexes is utterly inadequate and its results misleading.

lowed in the repercussions of inflation, in the privations
and sufferings of the masses and, above all, in the virtual
destruction of the German middle-class. Implicit in this
was the undermining of the domestic market for consumers' goods. There could hardly be found any instance
of productive capacity restored or built up more directly
at the price of the destruction of its own market. Moreover, the expansion of activity in the inflation period,
stimulated by the incentive of advancing prices and rising
profits, was essentially one-sided. While in some fields
there was reconstruction, re-equipment, and expansion
or over-expansion, there were others which fell behind or
were altogether neglected. In this regard the history of
German agriculture is of interest. It is true that high
prices during the inflation period enabled agricultural producers to pay off mortgages, in addition to what they had
liquidated during the War. Then, under the revalorization
scheme put into force after the stabilization of the currency, the balance of the old debts was reduced to 25 per
cent of their value. Measures were also taken to restore
farm equipment and stock. Yet, agriculture lagged behind
industry in taking advantage of inflationary conditions to
bring plant and equipment up to date. In the final stages
of the inflation period industrial expansion was carried on
to a large extent at the expense of the farmer. Stabilization
was followed by a severe agricultural crisis, with heavy
distress sales of agricultural produce which showed the
pressing need for cash, since by this time no one had any

Broadly speaking, the costs of restoration under inflationary conditions
include all such resources as went into activities which would never have
been undertaken except under the stimulus of inflation as being too
costly and economically unsound.

of the happy illusions induced by high paper prices.[7] The
new agricultural indebtedness grew rapidly, caused by the
need for meeting current operating expenses, taxes, interest,
or merely the purchase of necessary supplies.

By the end of 1931 the agricultural mortgages amounted
to 5,850 million marks, as compared with 13 billion marks
at the end of 1913;[8] in other words, in seven post-stabilization years — the years in which foreign observers thought
of Germany as a land of rapidly increasing prosperity —
the agricultural section of the population had piled up a
debt which amounted to fully 45 per cent of the total
which had accumulated throughout long generations before the War. Moreover, to the farm indebtedness of
Germany were added short-term obligations which by
1929 reached a total estimated at about 4,400 million marks.
While the principal of this debt was still much smaller
than before the War, the burden of its charges was relatively
much heavier, as the interest rate was about twice as high.

This matter of high interest rates, due to shortage of
capital, was one of the outstanding problems of the entire
post-stabilization "recovery" period. It affords a striking
illustration of the illusory nature of the recovery which
was assumed to be under way; for it was a direct consequence of the way in which expansion under inflation
depleted resources through predatory exploitation at home
and ruinous sales abroad. Physically, restoration in the
leading industries was an accomplished fact, but economically it immobilized resources in plants which could

---

[7] Beckmann, in *Strukturwandlungen*, I, pp. 136–146; Friedrich Aereboe,
Der Einfluss des Krieges auf die landwirtschaftliche Produktion (Carnegie Endowment Series), Berlin, 1927, pp. 113 ff.

[8] Hugh Dalton and others, *Unbalanced Budgets*, p. 121.

not be operated at sufficiently low cost to secure liquid funds; thus a problem which was basic in industrial finance at the end of the War had been disguised by the inflation, but now reappeared again. Hence, a further reorganization of industry was found necessary, the one which was characterized by what was called the "rationalization" plans for lowering operating costs. It was this economy in management which brought Germany's industry farthest along the path of recovery; but capital was lacking for its full development and interest rates were high, further depleting liquid funds and increasing indebtedness, domestic and foreign. "Thus," says Dr. A. Gourvitch, whose analysis of this situation we have been following,[9] "Germany, even after stabilization, was still confronted with the problem of securing adequate cost levels and was still without the means of solving it. If the test of stabilization as an agency of recovery was to be the ability of the national economy to operate at definite price levels and under a definite system of price relationships, it did not stand the test.[10] It was only by borrowing ever more heavily, no

[9] In an analysis of the effect of the War upon Germany, made for the Endowment under the author's direction. The last three pages follow it closely.

[10] Dr. Gourvitch points out, in this connection, that, "as the devaluation of the currency meant a break in the continuity of calculations, all assets were subject to a revaluation, for which there was no certain basis. One of the legal measures which accompanied stabilization was that requiring all corporations to convert their balance sheets to a gold mark basis. This proved an exceedingly painful process. (See the discussion in W. Prion, *Kapital und Betrieb. Finanzierungsfragen der deutschen Wirtschaft*, Leipzig, 1929, pp. 12–16.) Valuation could be based upon prospective earnings only, whereas no forecast whatsoever could properly be made as to the movement either of the costs of production or of sales prices. The economic history of Germany since stabilization may be viewed as a record of vain attempts to fix costs and prices in a way largely arbitrary; this refers to wages in particular, which in 1924 were established by the employers in the leading industries at levels considerably below those of pre-war years, without regard to current or pro-

matter what this might cost or whether repayment of the debt could be assured, that most industrial enterprises were able to continue to operate and rationalize."

In 1929 Germany's industrial corporations were borrowing twice as much, compared to their tangible assets, as had been the case before the War, although the ratio had been notoriously high in Germany even then. Before the War the average interest charge against borrowed capital had been 4 per cent, while the net profit rate was twice as high; now the interest rate averaged 10 per cent and the average profit rate was under 5. This is not the whole story. The cash holdings in commercial bank assets, as compared with liabilities, was less than one half of the pre-war ratio. Moreover, the entire structure of bank credit depended upon the availability of foreign funds.

Two things should be clear from this short sketch of the history of post-war Germany: In the first place, all generalizations are false which are based on the period prior to the Great Depression, — that series of liquidations of the post-war credit structure; in the second place, all the apparent prosperity of the late Twenties was rendered hollow by the continuing effects of the War, accentuated by the Reparation and other Treaty payments. We shall see in a later chapter that the problem of this continuing disturbance was psychological as well as economic and that by far the largest part of the burden was War cost rather

---

spective costs of living, and with the inevitable necessity of sharp advances in the years to follow. The situation was quite analogous in the case of other cost items. Hence, between 1924 and 1927, the book values of corporate assets had, in many instances, to be repeatedly revised. It was the contention of Prion, probably the most thoughtful student of German financial problems, that German industry had nevertheless gradually adjusted itself to a new scale of values. In the light of subsequent developments, however, it may well be questioned whether any actual adjustment ever materialized."

than Treaty cost. But the failure to understand these things at the time, the almost universal belief that Germany was once more strongly on its feet and that the whole vast deficit had miraculously disappeared, this belief, due to a misunderstanding of war economics, strengthened the reluctance of Germany's creditors under the Treaty to cancel their obligations. If Germany was prospering, as seemed outwardly to be the case, if its standard of living was 15 per cent above that of pre-war Germany and its shipping and commerce were again threatening to outstrip those of other nations, and if its credit was inviting a flow of American investments, — why should it not meet with relative ease the Treaty payments which it had met in the past under much less favorable circumstances? Since no one could foretell in 1928 how much the prosperity of Germany as well as other countries rested on a false basis of over-expanded credit sooner or later to be liquidated, the policy of fulfilment of the Treaty of Versailles seemed economically and financially sound. But psychologically it kept alive the national resentment which had grown so strong in the hard years preceding and accentuated it in that section of the nation which did not share in the false prosperity of 1928.

This was the kind of situation which breeds revolution. For history has clearly shown that revolutions do not happen, or at least do not succeed, when a people is on the downward path, but only after it has turned the corner on its misfortunes and has started upward again. For example, the economic hardships of France under the old regime were worse than at the time of the Revolution. The Bolshevik Revolution is another case in point. It is when the oppressed and those who think themselves oppressed — which in the history of politics amounts to the same thing — begin to feel enough strength to make headway against oppressive conditions that movements for redress have to be reckoned with, because they begin to speak in terms of power. By intuition and instinct rather than any intelligent knowledge of these facts the greatest demagogue in Germany's history framed these resentments in terms of the Nazi revolt against the existing political system both at home and abroad.

The lesson for statesmanship in the rise of Hitler's Empire is not to be found in his explosive diatribes but in the failure of both the political and the business worlds to appreciate how necessary it is for every worthy citizen to have his share in the prosperity of a national economy, and that prosperity based too largely on borrowing stimulates hopes that cannot be realized, stirs resentments at their failure, and opens the door to those who substitute force for the plighted word.

CHAPTER V

THE TRADITION OF MILITARISM

So far we have been tracing the War and its aftermath in the material fortunes of the German people. But, as we have seen, even more disastrous was the ultimate effect upon its spiritual life. This is even more difficult to trace than the economic post-war history, for opinions and morals are the hardest to trace of all human possessions.[1] Although on the one hand they are rooted in habit and immemorial custom and therefore are in some ways more stable than material property, on the other hand at times they seem almost to be shifted from their base by the storm pressures of emotion. Nowhere is this dual character of a nation's outlook more evident than in Germany in the post-war years, as the following short sketch will show.

As the War drew to a close the German people found that the fortitude and desperate effort of four years of totalitarian struggle had brought them not only defeat but utter exhaustion. The continuance of the blockade throughout the cruel winter of 1918–19 drove them still further to despair. In their eyes there seemed no reason for the continuance of the blockade unless it was intended

---

[1] This fact became so evident in the making of *The Economic and Social History of the World War*, referred to in Chapter VIII, that the sociological section was finally narrowed down to a study of criminology because the violations of law offered a basis of statistical measurement not possible in the estimate of moral forces.

to crush them still further and bring them to a state of absolute powerlessness. The fact that peace had not yet been made and that Europe was living under the terms of a truce called an Armistice seemed to them but a quibble on the part of the Allied Powers, for no one really believed that Germany could take up arms again after having laid them down. The fact that the meeting of the Allied and Associated Powers in Paris was popularly known as a peace conference further strengthened the feeling that the war was over, although it did not legally come to a close until the Treaty of Peace was ratified in the following winter.

Under these conditions, the long delay in sending food to the half-starved Germans strengthened their sense of suffering by adding to it the feeling that all the world was still their enemy. The blockade was ultimately removed in March, some nine months before the Treaty was finally ratified and peace definitely established, but the damage to the spirit of Germany had already been done. A psychosis of self-pity swept over it which was destined to grow rather than lessen as the post-war years failed to restore prosperity to a world that had been both ruined and shell-shocked by the war.

This state of mind was aggravated by Germany's isolation from the rest of the world — a state of affairs which continued to a surprising degree during the first years after the war. While this was chiefly due to the barriers to international trade disordered by the fact of having only a poor or worthless currency, it was also due to the trend of German education of the pre-war days which had concentrated upon the great themes of German political unification and the triumphs of German science. No other nation had more to be proud of in the years which had just passed into history before the great catastrophe of the

World War. German nationalism was wounded at the height of its pride; and when self-centered nationalism is so beaten down and humiliated, it takes defeat doubly to heart because it has never developed the capacity, nor even the wish, for understanding how other people have suffered from the effects of war. This leads directly towards a pathological state of mind which is ready to believe that the nation is the victim — and it goes without saying, the innocent victim — of the special malice of its foes.

The extent to which Germany remained spiritually isolated from other nations as a consequence of the World War was one of the most real influences in the political life of the Republic. Passing mention has been made in the preceding pages of the difficulties which the newly established German Treasury encountered in the collection of taxes. The German industrialists and bankers who connived at tax evasion or deliberately resorted to it had no idea how bravely and with what sacrifice British capital was attempting to meet the cost of the War to Britain. I recall an evening spent in the winter of 1923 with a group of the great industrial leaders of Germany in which they frankly stated their complete ignorance of how the war had affected the economy of any other country than their own. This was at a time when, owing to the catastrophic sinking of the mark, the actual taxes collected from a great automobile factory with some two hundred acres of plant was the equivalent of one automobile; so much had the money depreciated between the time of assessment and the time of collection. While the country as a whole suffered, the owner of the plant escaped paying within many thousand times what the English industrialist was then forced to meet in taxes. But of all the economic hardships suffered by business in other countries German business knew little and cared less, for war psychology still left its echo in the isolationist complex.

The tradition of militarism was also responsible for keeping the German people ignorant of what the War was costing other countries. Although we know now that the conquests of the Central Powers and the use of the occupied territory brought them far less than had been confidently hoped for, it was still a commonplace of thinking that victory meant advantage; therefore, it was taken for granted that the victorious powers were suffering far less than the vanquished. The theory of war that was expressed in the Treaties of Brest-Litovsk and Bucharest is blind to the real nature of totalitarian war which makes victory delusive by the exhaustion of the victor. Those who thought in these terms could hardly imagine what was happening in England at that time, how hopeless seemed the problem of its unemployment, how much the markets of its world trade had vanished or what a burden of taxation was falling upon the propertied classes. Viewed through the misty distance of the North Sea, England was fortunate and relatively happy, while Germany was struggling under the burden of its defeat and the apprehension of revolution. That this picture was false did not affect the situation so far as the German attitude of mind was concerned. The fact that war was no longer the simple process by which one nation gained advantage from another and built its prosperity upon the exploitation of its spoil — that fact was as yet not clearly seen by those who were bred in the tradition of Frederick the Great; for the older militarism still left its mark not only upon soldiers but upon reactionary statesmen down to 1918. In the revival of militarism today it does not speak so loudly owing to the sobered mood of those who lived through the World War, but it is still the essence of militarism, however limited and qualified by the lessons of experience.

It is impossible to say how much the military tradition of Prussia affected the outlook of the German people in the years following the World War. There is no doubt that the Spartan trend in the Prussian training which exalts the army in the eyes of civilians lent a touch of romance to even the sordid spectacle of impoverishment and suffering when caused by "military necessity." If the soldier was ready to sacrifice his life in the field, it was but fitting that the civilian should accept as a part of his patriotic duty the minor sacrifices which fell to his lot. This sentiment of solidarity is shared more or less by all nations at war, even by those which admit it with reluctance. But nowhere else has it developed to a cult which pervades the whole conception of citizenship as has been the case in Germany. Here we come upon one of the historic roots of the philosophy of militant Nazism; for militarism had been a real instrument in the upbuilding of Prussia and of German unity. In the years following the war it was the fashion for liberal writers in other countries, especially in America, to protest that this conception of Germany was unfair and untrue, a legacy of war-time propaganda. Had the liberals confined their efforts to a study of ways and means for preventing a recrudescence of militarism, instead of pretending that the danger of it did not exist, they would have been more helpful to Germany and to the world, for the young German Republic that sought to escape from the clutches of the past was only too well aware of the continuing strength of that tradition which, for the time being, was in eclipse. When our liberals surrendered to false sentimentality and failed to discriminate between militaristic and truly democratic movements within the Reich, as most of them did throughout the decade of the twenties, they lessened the strength of their liberating movement both in Germany and outside it.

Judged in the light of history there was nothing sinister in the fact that militarism had played so large a part in Prussian and German history. After all, what the German Empire owed to the army was no more than what the British Empire owed to its navy or what American unity owed to the armies of the North. The kingdom which the Hohenzollern founded, and around which the small and weak states of Northern Germany were drawn together, was a frontier country on the edge of the great stretches where semi-Asiatic peoples long threatened their security. The Hohenzollern kingship of Prussia was the outgrowth of the conquests of the crusading Knights of the Teutonic Order. A feudal land-owning aristocracy along that frontier maintained the military tradition from that day to this. The rigid discipline and sense of duty in army training furnished an example as well for the civilian bureaucracy which, from the days of the Great Elector, proved to be an invaluable instrument of peace-time autocratic rule. Bureaucracy and militarism therefore worked hand in hand serving the same ends. And when the forces of liberalism and democracy began to speak a different language, from 1848 to 1862, the old order found a champion in Bismarck who, by brow-beating the Prussian Diet and deliberately choosing the way of "blood and iron" instead of "speeches and resolutions," determined the course of German history, with fateful consequences for all the world. Bismarck himself was fully conscious, at the time, of the epochal importance of the decision. As he urged his King, William I, to defy Parliament by appealing to him as the first officer of the Prussian Army, his mind went back to the days of Charles I of England, a king who never swerved from his duty but "sealed his royal intent with his blood."

The heir of that historic event was Adolf Hitler, for not only did Bismarck win but he taught the German people to lose confidence in themselves, as a people lacking in political capacity. No nation can honestly say that of itself because capacity is not the gift of race but an outgrowth of circumstance and breeding. It must be remembered, however, that Bismarck himself, as long as he was in power, held in check the militarism he had invoked, and that the first principle of his statesmanship was to maintain civilian control of policies of state. Unfortunately for Germany there was but one Bismarck.

The effect of the World War upon the German people has to be considered in the light of this history. They had been taught to think of war as a necessary instrument of policy and were trained not to let their sentimentality temper its iron rigors. But the World War was different. Victory in the field had availed nothing. The fact that German war-time propaganda had maintained the conviction in public opinion that the army had never been defeated in battle made the ultimate disaster inexplicable in terms of pure military history. As the armies marched home in their final retreat from the Western Front, even they began to share the common feeling that they had been invincible. Tired and demoralized at first, the soldiers' spirits rose as they marched back through the large cities to be greeted by cheering crowds and have garlands hung on their rifles; the more the trenches were left behind, the more readily they accepted the plaudits that are ordinarily accorded to victorious troops. But the dead weight of privation was still upon them and upon the cheering cities through which they passed. Here was something which history could not explain; victory in the field had brought only the fruits of defeat. They all faced the fundamental and unescapable fact that Germany was a ruined nation in a world it had helped to ruin. Somewhere, someone or something was to blame. But who, or what?

At first the blame for what had happened was placed squarely upon the government of Imperial Germany, especially the Kaiser and, to a less degree, his chancellor, Bethmann-Hollweg. The conviction that they had at least blundered into war began to grow in the middle class and found lodgment even among conservatives as well; while the Socialists, now for the first time brought into the precincts of power, saw at close range the justification of their belief that the Prussian militarists of Berlin had joined with the Hapsburg reactionaries of Vienna to force the war upon their own peace-loving peoples as well as upon those of other nations. We shall see later that they were nearer to the truth in this than those who subsequently carried the day against them by the organized propaganda of the war-guilt movement which sought to put the blame upon others. The point here, however, is not how much of the responsibility for causing the war really should fall upon the governments of the Central Powers in 1914, but how the German people felt about this in 1918. Opening the archives of the German Foreign Office, they found enough evidence to show that the German Government had not been frank with the world, to say the least, in its publication of war-time documents. The German White Book of August 1914, which purported to contain the essential diplomatic documents on the part that Germany played in the outbreak of the war had contained only some 27 documents, and there was nothing of the exchanges between

Berlin and Vienna, the most important of all in judging Germany's case. The White Book which the German Republic now produced contained no less than 1,123 documents, with no reservation. This was begun partly as an act of revolution against the former German Government; but whatever animus there may have been in the criticism of Kautsky, the Socialist member of the commission that produced the book, it was checked by the technical competence of his colleagues, the former General Montgelas and Professor Schücking, an outstanding European figure in the field of international law. So strong did the current of attack run against the old Government of Germany that a commission was appointed by the Reichstag of the Republic to investigate the responsibilities of the Emperor's Government.[2] While these proceedings published in 1920 throw some light upon what happened in Berlin and Potsdam in 1914, they leave the issue unsettled; for the evidence bore only upon the acts of one government, and to assign responsibility for a war one must be able to examine both parties to the conflict.

The evidence of the former Chancellor Bethmann-Hollweg before this commission contains a passage that throws a flood of light upon the trend of German opinion in the year following the war. Feeling keenly the fact that he was on the defensive, and that wide circles in Germany blamed him as well as the Kaiser for having caused the war by incompetence or deliberate acts, he pointed out that the attitude towards war itself had changed as a result of the World War, and that to judge the statesmanship of 1914 by the standards of international morality

---

[2] The proceedings of this investigation were published by the Carnegie Endowment for International Peace in 1923 under the title *Official German Documents Relating to the World War*.

which Germany along with the rest of the world was attempting to establish in 1920, was to falsify the judgment of history, because the statesmen of 1914 had no such standards to go upon. Bethmann-Hollweg went on to challenge the pacifist trend of the day to provide any other solution than war for a situation like that which Austria faced after the murder of the Archduke; but his defense of power politics only brought out in still clearer light the revolt against that method of settling Europe's disputes, of which there was plenty of evidence, in the years immediately following the War, in German literature and journalism as well as in the debates of the Reichstag. This protest against war naturally found strongest voice in labor circles, but it resulted in national peace movements, the first important political movements of the kind in German history. That is not to say that it was foreign to German thought and culture. Parallel with German militarism there had always existed a strong love of peace in the hearts of the German people. German thinkers have had their full share in framing theories of international peace, and their contributions in this field should be kept in mind alongside those of the theorists of nationalism. Nowhere else in literature is there a nobler challenge to human conduct than in the little classic Immanuel Kant wrote on Eternal Peace (*Zum Ewigen Frieden*) almost a century and a half ago; but the challenge never became the slogan of the German people until the Hohenzollern made way for the Republic.

Naturally the sentiment against war was strongest where the sufferings of war had been most felt, in the rank and file of the German people; and its thoroughgoing protest against militarism swelled to notable proportions. The anniversary of the outbreak of the war in August 1914

was recalled with something of the same poignant feeling
as Armistice Day in the Allied countries, and German labor
added a note of challenge to war itself, as the instrument
of death and disaster, when at vast public meetings it
gathered under the slogan "NEVER WAR AGAIN" (*nie wieder
Krieg*). Under the shadow of Bismarck's monument, in
front of the parliament house in Berlin, it joined with more
moderate political groups to give voice to the anxious hope
that the Republic should stand for the new era of human
understanding, which would constitute an even greater
revolution in human affairs than that which had sup-
planted autocracy by democratic government.

The ultimate failure of this movement inside Germany
was a catastrophe for the world greater than any defeat in
battle which history registers. The chief reason for it
was that, as time went on and the War receded into
memory, the continuing distress and suffering of the
German people were felt to have a more definite cause
in the immediate present, while the past was ever growing
more remote. The evils of the day were attributed to the
peace-time policies and to the malevolence of Germany's
neighbors. Unfortunately, the post-war policies of these
neighbors were of a kind to justify much of this reaction in
Germany; and as the whole international polity of Europe,
so far as it affected Germany, was conditioned by the
Treaty of Versailles, it was perhaps inevitable that the explanation for Germany's ills should more and more be
transferred from a revulsion against war to a continuing
stubborn conflict over the fulfilment or non-fulfilment
of the terms of the peace treaty.

It is an over-simplification of history to say simply that
the peace movement was submerged in the war-guilt controversy, although that is what ultimately took place.

It is doubtful if this path which led to Hitler would have been entered upon if German pacification had been taken at its full value in other countries. Unfortunately, war devastates confidence in the good faith of an adversary, and this is sometimes even harder to restore than the property that has been destroyed. The difficulty is increased when foreign affairs become a subject of democratic debate. French and British public opinion, therefore, was never quite sure whether the German peace movement was genuine or only a passing phase or perhaps even a camouflage of diplomacy for the purposes of disarming the opposition to a revision of the Treaty of Peace. This failure of the peace movement in other countries to appreciate the possibilities in Germany is an outstanding fact which, however understandable, relieves Germany of much of the blame for what happened when its peace movement really became the expression of an impotent minority.

It is almost impossible to weave the tangled threads of German post-war opinion into any consistent pattern because of the confusion in which it was left by the economic, moral and political displacement of the War. But the strength of the sentiment for peace may be gauged at least in part by the support of the "policy of fulfilment" of the Treaty of Versailles, which was the keynote of German foreign relations until Hitler's accession to power in 1933. It was not easy to cling to a pacific policy when peace seemed to be offering Germany so little. Nevertheless when it came to a choice between the *status quo* and a resort to war, none of the Central Powers, not even Hungary which had suffered most in the Treaty of Peace, was ready to plunge Europe into anarchy, which is what resort to war would have meant. Germany shared this feeling to the full, and as early as the autumn of 1922 Chancellor Cuno, on the advice or at least with the friendly support of the American Ambassador, Alanson B. Houghton, offered a positive step towards peace by proposing a thirty year truce between France and Germany on the basis of the *status quo*. The German Government was unable to secure the good offices of Secretary Hughes as the intermediary to present this offer to the British and French Governments, and when Bonar Law, having been apprised of it, mentioned the offer to Poincaré in their meeting in Paris, it was regarded only as a diplomatic manoeuvre to stave off the exactions of the Allies. Mr. Elihu Root's judgment on this incident — given at the time — is worth recalling, for it was that the world so lacked confidence in Germany's good faith that any proposition emanating from it at that time would not be taken as sincere. In any case, that was what happened. Poincaré carried the day and the French went into the Ruhr. There is no doubt that the German Government of 1922 that made this offer to France did hope thereby to have the burden of reparations lightened, and it seems quite clear that Cuno's own thought had been more like that of a bargaining business man than of a constructive statesman. Moreover, the great industrialists, whom he — as former general manager of the Hamburg-American Line — represented in political life, were by no means the best organs for a pacific gesture like this. Nevertheless the Cuno offer was real; discounted and rejected, it was later to furnish the materials with which Stresemann could build the foundations of the Treaties of Locarno.

The history of the Stresemann era is too large a theme to be dealt with here, but it is one of which Germany has every reason to be proud. It was a message from him in the Cologne Gazette which enabled Austen Chamberlain to set going the negotiations that resulted in the Locarno

Treaties. But even more than formal engagements, was the change in attitude toward Germany and its needs, which was beginning to make possible at last a pacific Europe. Slowly, but as fast as shell-shocked Europe was ready to move, the harshest clauses of the Treaty of Versailles were being either modified or broken down. Contrary to popular opinion, the Republic had succeeded by its policy of fulfilment or by its persistent and unyielding opposition, in freeing Germany from practically all of the "servitudes" of the Treaty, except the rectification of boundaries. This is, of course, a very large exception, but frontiers would mean less if those behind them were co-operative and friendly. The Hitler method of territorial revision by the threat or use of force, robs the economy of Europe of any permanent prosperity, and without the prosperity of Europe, Germany itself cannot prosper.

However one may judge the success or failure of the diplomacy of the German democratic Republic, the fact remains that down to its close it was based upon the presumption of peace. In 1927 I had an opportunity to observe the attitude of the German Government toward the fundamental question of the validity of the use of war as an instrument of policy, that old familiar doctrine of German militarism. The inaugural lecture which, on assuming the Carnegie Endowment professorship I delivered at the *Hochschule für Politik*, was devoted to the thesis that the World War had proved that war was no longer a pertinent instrument of policy, because of the interdependence of world economy. It was a gratifying experience to find that not only German statesmen but the greatest of her soldiers as well held my point of view, which was a conclusion drawn from years of study in connection with the preparation of the *Economic and Social History of the World*

War. If these conclusions were true, however, it followed that to turn to war as an instrument of policy would henceforth be an act of criminal folly on the part of the statesmen of any civilized country. Out of this followed the further conclusion stated in terms of an American slogan, "the outlawry of war." In 1927, in spite of all disturbing and distracting problems, German statesmanship was as ready to take up and apply this principle as that of any other country.

This is not the place to develop in detail the origins of what later became popularly known as the Kellogg-Briand Pact. But its basic principle (*Machtpolitik* is no longer *Realpolitik*), that politics of power is no longer practical and calculable by nations which have become interdependent in their economic life, was first set forth in Berlin before it was taken up by Briand. Paris was chosen as the place for launching the plan of an international agreement because the experience of the Cuno offer showed that such a proposal would be still suspect if coming from the successors of Bismarck. Such a denial of traditional Prussian statecraft was too bold and novel to be readily accepted unless there had been full preparation for it by public discussion and diplomatic exchanges. But, looking back over the subsequent history of the Peace Pact, it is not too much to say that the members of the German Government from the Chancellor down, showed in their private discussions as keen a sense of both the necessity of and the difficulty in the elimination of war as an instrument of national policy as did those governments which actually negotiated it. Thus, as late as 1927, the German Government, in spite of its preoccupation with post-war problems, was still responsive to the final lesson of the World War.

Few governments in history have suffered more at the

hands of their own people than that of the German Republic, and the rest of the world has perforce largely subscribed to their judgment. This was the first success of Nazi propaganda, that poison compounded of envy and malice toward all the agencies of peace and enlightenment. The public, not discriminating between this type of virulent blackmail and the ordinary criticism which is the life of politics, lent a willing ear to the charge that the leaders of democratic Germany were not only incompetent but false to the great traditions of the Reich. History has already shown that the treason to Germany lay solely in the treachery of the conspirators. But in their task of convincing Germany of the contrary, they succeeded so well that few Germans, even those who are refugees in other lands from the Nazi terror, are ready to do justice to the statesmanship which staggered under the load left by the World War.

It does not seem to have occurred to those who hold such a low opinion of the government of Republican Germany that this opinion was the argument of rebels and therefore in its very nature less a judgment than a prejudice. It was a prejudice, however, which, as we have seen, has Bismarckian history behind it; but it was strengthened as well by a complex of inferiority with reference to the English, whom they regarded as endowed with a native political capacity which had been denied the Germans as a birthright. This belief was adopted, almost as an article of faith, by historians and statesmen, alike utterly oblivious of the fact that every other nation — not excluding the British — is critical of its government and that its dissatisfaction is generally in proportion to its education and maturity. Nowhere else is there a lower opinion expressed of politics and politicians than in France, unless it be in the United States. Political capacity is not a racial or even a natural gift. It is the application of intelligence to problems which lie beyond the range of any one generation and need the experience of history for their solution. History has denied the German people that experience except to a limited degree and at rare intervals, but the government of the Republic showed as much innate capacity for dealing with problems of state as the German industrialists showed in dealing with the problems of organized industry. It was not a mere chance that a saddler, Ebert, guided the infant Republic with such courage and intelligence as to win the confidence of even his conservative opponents, or that a representative of the middle class, like Bruening, should prove for a few short years a worthy successor of Bismarck. The myth that Germans lack political capacity is not borne out by the history of the post-war years, in spite of the fact that the government failed to undo the damage that had been caused by the War. That was a task utterly beyond human capacity, but the seeds of sedition ripened into a harvest of hatred for all that the democratic Republic stood for: honesty, freedom, and even-handed justice both at home and abroad.

The more one looks back upon the effort of Germany to find itself in the troubled post-war world, the more one's sympathy grows for those who failed. Whether Germany would have reverted in time to its pre-war militarism or not is a question that no one can answer. The weakness of the Republic in allowing political organizations to appear in uniform and under military discipline, its connivance at their secret arming, its failure to adjust taxation equitably, its extravagance in order to quiet social unrest, all might perhaps have been overcome had not the last economic result of the war swept over the world in the great depression, which ruined markets, paralyzed commerce, and wrecked finance. In spite of all these difficulties, however, the disciplined spirit of the German people might have been counted upon to keep them at least from falling behind in the path of political progress. A nation which could, by an act of faith, make believe that the Rentenmark of 1923 was really money and make it a sound currency, when it violated every law of national banking, had possibilities of leadership in political as well as social emancipation. But Germany was lost because it accepted a false doctrine based upon a national act of forgetfulness. A single explanation was offered for Germany's ills which obscured the past as it was to falsify the future. The Treaty of Versailles became more and more the symbol of a political movement which centered upon the task of deliverance. Growingly impatient at obstruction and delay, public opinion tended to doubt more and more the policy of fulfilment, and then, opening the gates of revolution, turned back to militarism. This last fateful move was the sign that the lesson of the World War had now been completely forgotten. The deliverer who was to lead Germany back to its place in the sun turned the mind of the German people from seeking liberation from the servitudes of war to seeking it from the servitudes of a treaty. And the method of liberation was that which the World War had shown to be a fundamental basis of any nation's servitudes, — a return to militarism.

CHAPTER VI

WAR GUILT

In all the history of propaganda nothing outrivals the success of the German effort against the Treaty of Versailles. The easy triumph of this propaganda in Germany itself might be taken for granted, for reasons stated here; but the conquest of German opinion, which swung it away from the war to the attack upon the Treaty, was only the strategic base from which its larger compaign was carried on in other countries. Strengthened by sincere conviction and moving with unswerving purpose the crusaders for Germany's case were able to mobilize liberal opinion everywhere for the denunciation of the Treaty as the continuing embodiment of that war psychology which liberalism inherently abhors. Few crusades have been so favored; for the Treaty supplied ammunition for the attack upon it and it fitted in with the post-war swing of public opinion away from war-time leadership. The reaction against the regimentation necessary for winning a war was all the stronger in the United States because the causes of the war had seemed so remote from anything in America's past history. Even after three years of European fighting the entry of the United States into the War in 1917 came as an emotional shock to those whose minds would normally have been most aware of the dangers of American involvement. I mean those public-spirited citizens who were devoting their lives to social betterment and the war against corruption in our cities. They rightly saw that most, if not all, of their cherished plans would suffer eclipse if the United States were to concentrate all its energy upon correcting European and world affairs instead of combating the evils at home. Resentment at having to embark upon such an alien enterprise had colored their thinking throughout the three years of American neutrality, which seemed doubly justified by the European nature of the conflict and the interests of America itself. When, in 1917, the unlimited submarine warfare of Germany broke down the defenses of American neutrality, American liberalism accepted the challenge; but the irritation of having to do so continued subconsciously and made it an unsparing critic of its war-time leader, Wilson, as soon as the War was succeeded by diplomacy.

From 1919 to 1939 this liberalism cherished its wounds and gave vent to the animosities which it had suppressed. It was therefore a willing and ready victim for those who could exploit its prejudices and, stirred by its emotional complex, it accepted with barely superficial examination the hostile political attack upon the peace treaties in the United States Senate, — an attack based upon principles that were the very opposite to liberalism, and offering nothing designed to free international relations from the continuing menace of war. If anyone doubts this, let him read that least read of all our treaties of peace, the one which we signed with Germany, the Treaty of Berlin of 1921.

By a strange paradox, moreover, the opposition of Senator Lodge and his associates to the Treaty came to be thought of as substantially on the same basis as that of those who accused the makers of the Treaty of being too harsh with Germany. Even today most people seem to think that the Treaty which the United States made was more liberal than the Treaty of Versailles; as a matter of fact, it retained all of America's interests in the Versailles Treaty and removed from it only the reference to the League of Nations and the International Labor Office which Wilson had fought for as the means for ultimately liberating a world which was not yet ready for full and free coöperation among nations. Few have ever read the Treaty of Berlin by which the United States made peace with Germany. For that matter few of those who have protested most against the Treaty of Versailles have ever read more than the smallest fraction of it. The controversy is one in which ignorance combines with higher and generous motives to distort the truth and falsify the outlook.

I have told the story elsewhere of what happened at the Paris Peace Conference,[1] and my analysis of how the Treaty was made and the reasons for it has been accepted by both my former colleagues at the conference and the historians who are now engaged in studying it. An examination of how the Treaty was actually made shows what a travesty of history it is to picture those who made it as a set of vindictive men intent only upon the ruin of the German people. We have already alluded to the fact that Wilson's opposition in Congress was for a "sterner justice" than the Treaty. But it is not generally known in America that Clemenceau failed to be elected to the presidency of France chiefly because in French public opinion he had not taken enough guarantees against Germany. As for Lloyd George and his British colleagues in Paris, the fact is well established now that they fully realized before the conference was over the need for the revision of the Treaty by lightening the burden upon the Central Powers. It was

[1] *At the Paris Peace Conference*, New York, The Macmillan Company, 1937.

apprehension of political opposition back home which more than any other influence prevented the statesmen in Paris from recasting, in part at least, the terms of the Treaty. This fact, which was well known to all of us who lived through the experience of the Peace Conference, was one of the obscure but potent elements in preventing a negotiated peace. Again, as in every other phase of this history, the war itself was to blame; for wars are not over when the firing stops. They continue in the form of distrust and animosity which paralyse sound judgment and make that supreme quality of statesmanship — generosity based upon understanding — almost impossible.

Those who drafted the treaties of peace were not a conclave of conspirators against the peace of Europe, or its prosperity and happiness. They were dealing with a world in which, across the ruin of three great empires — Hohenzollern, Hapsburg and Romanoff — voices of freedom were making themselves heard partly in terms of anarchy but partly in the familiar notes of political liberty for oppressed peoples. The response to this call was as confused as the call itself. The restoration of Poland and the acceptance of Masaryk's philosophy — based as it was on Jeffersonian democracy — were acts of which the Peace Conference had every reason to be proud; but those who set the boundaries for these new liberties were concerned more, in the strategic sense, with the pre-war state of Europe than with writing a charter for a new era. It was a political blunder not to secure for them a more friendly neighborhood in Central Europe into which their new sovereignties were thrust. But anyone who ever visited, at Konopischt, the home of the murdered Archduke Franz Ferdinand and compared it with the home of Masaryk would get a sense of what the dissolution of the Austrian Empire meant to its subject peoples. In the castle of the Archduke every room bristled with armament and was adorned with the mounted heads of the victims of his hunt, thousands of them, while Masaryk's summer home was a school-teacher's house in a peasant village. The dining room had as its only ornaments a wall map of Czecho-Slovakia and one of the United States. Not a single soldier in uniform was to be seen in the neighborhood. This was indeed a contrast between the old and the new; and yet, the transition was too great, the responsibilities of government had not been fully learned. The treaties of peace, although they sought to safeguard the rights of minorities, left unsolved problems too difficult for even the wisest of statesmen to grapple with.

It is not possible here to deal with the peace settlement in all its varied detail. That would require an analysis not only of the greatest collection of treaties ever made at one time but also a knowledge of the past history of all the peoples involved and the subsequent history of Europe. All that can be said in this short survey is that no one has a right to pronounce a final judgment upon the work of the Paris Peace Conference who is ignorant of the facts in the case. Unfortunately even the main facts have been misstated and misunderstood. Some of these must be dealt with here.

The Paris Peace Conference never really met. It was only a Preliminary Peace Conference of the Allied and Associated Powers which met at Paris in January, 1919, for the purpose of agreeing upon the terms of peace to be offered to Germany. It was an effort to seek agreement on one side of a council table so as to prevent the repetition of what had happened at the Congress of Vienna a century earlier, when Talleyrand was able to create division among the allies that had fought Napoleon. The real Peace Conference should have met, as everyone knows now, when the Germans were invited to come to Versailles to receive the terms of a treaty which the Allies had agreed upon. Had that meeting taken place, there is no doubt that the Treaty of Versailles would have been modified, because there was already plenty of evidence of division of opinion. The movement for revision was most vociferous in the American Delegation, but only among the unimportant minor officials; it was strong enough in the British Delegation to cause Lloyd George to threaten to tear up some of the agreements, especially with reference to the Polish Corridor. This discontent in Paris with the proposed terms of peace showed itself as soon as the whole treaty was put together from the reports of more than a dozen commissions which had been working separately, each at its own task. Had each of the sections of the treaty been all that there was, there would have been little to complain of, apart from Reparation and the Eastern Frontier.[2] But when all were added together — and this could not be done until all were completed — it was clear to most of us that it was too much to ask of any one country at any one time.

That is when the Peace Conference with the Germans should have met, but the opposition to Wilson in the United States would have fought more bitterly than any other political party anywhere the postponement of a settlement which would have inevitably followed from further negotiations with Germany. This state of mind was strengthened by the reports sent back home by American journalists who were either convinced opponents of Wilson themselves or were employed by newspapers of the opposition. Naturally, news of this situation reached

[2] On this see *At the Paris Peace Conference*, Chapter IV.

Berlin, and with a disastrous effect; for the German Government, shut off from direct contact with the Allied conclave, was led by this partisan attack upon Wilson to expect the worst. There was one source of Paris gossip which was especially followed in Berlin, messages sent out through the Lyons Wireless Station by Americans furnishing ammunition for Senator Lodge and his associates. This was sometimes spoken of as Senator Lodge's "private wire to the Peace Conference." From it the German Government got a distorted view of the whole proceeding, representing Wilson as the dupe of his associates, all of which, fitting in with its own apprehension, made it ready to believe the worst. This was a poor preparation for negotiation; caution in diplomacy is a first requisite; but when distrust goes so far as to presuppose failure, it leads to the mistakes in judgment which always follow upon a weakened morale.

Although the Germans at Versailles were badly treated, they must share with the Allies some of the blame for what happened. Their leader, Count Brockdorff-Rantzau, made two irreparable blunders. His failure to rise in addressing the ex-enemy governments was, as we know now, a planned discourtesy, and it was taken for what it was meant to be. But more important than this was the fact that, without having as yet read the text of the Treaty, then handed to him for the first time, he launched into a passionate denunciation of it. His information had been journalism and gossip of the kind just indicated, but he had as yet no official knowledge of the text of the Treaty, and by his vehement denunciation of it, closed the doors that might otherwise have been opened in part at least, owing to the division of opinion then prevailing on the other side of the table.

Germany, however, neither knew nor cared to know

how the Treaty of Versailles came to be what it was. The
easiest explanation was that the Allied statesmen, although
nominally under Wilson's leadership, had been carried
along by Clemenceau to a policy of post-war reprisal, the
sole purpose of which was the destruction of Germany.
This interpretation of what had happened was unquestioned
by all Germans, and was taught in the schools to the coming generation, who were to translate this belief into a
denial of democracy and all that it stood for.

The center of the protest which Germany made against
the Treaty of Versailles was what is called "the War Guilt
Controversy." There is no stranger chapter in history than
the use which was made of that diplomatic blunder which
forced Germany to subscribe to Article 231 of the Treaty.
That fateful article which was designed to furnish the
basis for Germany's "servitudes" in the Treaty of Versailles, but which was destined to be used for Germany's
ultimate advantage, read as follows:

> The Allied and Associated Governments affirm and Germany
> accepts the responsibility of Germany and her allies for caus-
> ing all the loss and damage to which the Allied and Associated
> Governments and their nationals have been subjected as a
> consequence of the war imposed upon them by the aggression
> of Germany and her allies.

From the very first moment when this text reached the
eyes of the German delegation at Versailles, it was interpreted by them as an accusation, an interpretation which
had not been intended by those who drafted it. It had not
been drafted as an accusation of moral guilt. It was just a
matter-of-fact basis for a legal claim. That it was only
intended in the latter sense is clear from the minutes and
notes of the commission which drafted it. In its first form

it entirely lacked the word "causing" so that the phrase read "that the Allied and Associated Governments affirm and Germany accepts the responsibility of Germany and her allies for all the loss and damage." That is merely a statement of financial obligation. The second part of the Article is not a part of the responsibility which Germany assumes. It is true it describes the War as one imposed upon the Allies by the aggression of Germany and her Allies, but that was a purely subsidiary clause and the Article as a whole was intended simply to state that Germany accepted the responsibility for loss and damage arising from a war which it and its allies had started. That Austria began the actual fighting first and that Germany's declaration of war preceded those of the Entente Powers were simple historical facts,[3] so the text of this whole Article might have been taken to mean that Germany shouldered the responsibility of paying for the damage created by a war in which the Central Powers had actually initiated the hostilities. The idea that Germany alone was to bear the whole responsibility was a natural interpretation of the text; but the same formula was inserted in the other treaties, and all it meant was that each of the signatories was a full partner in what they had jointly done. It must be remembered too, that the word "aggression" as used here had never been defined in international law, and indeed there are those who claim that it can never be defined at all. Therefore the way was open for the German Government to interpret the charge against it set forth in Article 231 in terms that would not involve any moral question of right or wrong but simply a statement of history. On the contrary their translation into

---

[3] This, of course, does not go to the bottom of the question, as all readers of the War Guilt literature know. The priority of mobilization has also to be considered. This, however, did not enter into the legal argument of the actual change from peace to a status of war.

German put Germany much more definitely in the wrong. The phrase "for causing" was translated *als Urheber,* thus making it read that Germany and her allies were responsible "as the prime cause" for all the loss and damage. This goes definitely beyond what either the French or English texts stated. In the French text, the phrase "for causing loss and damage" becomes a parenthesis "for having caused them," so that all that Germany accepts is the responsibility for the loss and damage and nothing more.

That is the way it could have been interpreted. But by the strangest of paradoxes, it was the Germans themselves who insisted both at Versailles and in subsequent years on putting the worst possible interpretation on the "war-guilt clause." They were induced thereto not only by the apparent ambiguity of the text, but also by the common knowledge that their enemies did really believe them guilty of aggression, an opinion justified by the correspondence with the Allies at Versailles, although the Treaty accused only the Kaiser, not Germany, of a "supreme offence against international morality and the law of nations." It was but a step from this interpretation of Article 231 to the final form in which the war-guilt thesis was stated popularly both in Germany and abroad, namely that the Treaty of Versailles had accused Germany not only of war-guilt, but of the sole guilt for the war. It is perhaps natural that those who feel themselves unjustly charged with wrong-doing should exaggerate the charge in their own minds; but when a nation acts this way, while it may in the long run bring greater discredit to the opposing governments, it blocks the path of compromise by making the two points of view so utterly irreconcilable. In this case it is not too much to say that had Germany interpreted Article 231 as a purely business statement instead of a moral denunciation, it could have held the issue down much more easily to the definite matter of capacity for payment, which was the only working basis for European recovery. Instead of doing this, Germany concentrated upon clearing what it regarded as the stain upon its reputation, attempting to prove the falsity of a charge that had never really been meant by the drafters of the text. The result was that in making out that the Treaty contained the most sweeping of indictments against it, Germany was able to rally to the support of its cause in the post-war years the majority of the liberal opinion of the allied countries as well. Never was propaganda more successful.

Now the question of responsibility for having started the war was a purely historical question. That was the first point made by those who attacked Article 231 claiming that the case against Germany had been pre-judged by its enemies. As we have seen, this was not what the Treaty set forth. But if that had been the case, the method pursued by the German critics of the Treaty was fully as unscientific as the first phase of the controversy in the autumn of 1914. Then the documents of history were used to win the war; now they were to win the peace. New documents were published; memoirs of statesmen and criticisms of historians began to appear in all the countries that had been engaged in the war; a society was founded to study the war-guilt question and a monthly magazine (*Die Kriegsschuldfrage*) to keep watch over all other publications in every land. The more distant origins of the war were not forgotten in the scholarly series of volumes containing the essential documents of the Foreign Office from 1870 to the World War. These efforts evoked similar activities in the ex-enemy countries until the output resembled that of the theological controversies of the sixteenth and seventeenth centuries when Protestants attacked and Catholics defended the prerogatives and history of the Papacy. In both cases the history was not the final aim but the means to another end, that of a justification of a cause. But one cannot seek the truth even for such uses without learning something of its reality.

The result of the controversy has been to enlarge our knowledge of pre-war diplomacy, but in the course of it every kind of fallacy in historical criticism has crept in and been used to the full, both consciously — by those with a case to prove, and unconsciously — by those whose training in such matters was insufficient to put them wholly upon their guard. For example, there are some who seem to think that the more documents they have, the safer their conclusions, without regard to the relative merit of the texts themselves. This fallacy of piling up citations is one of the commonest in historical research. Few can refuse themselves the satisfaction of accumulating a mass of documents bearing upon the subject in hand so as to be able to supply more citations in support of their conclusions or in opposition to those of their opponents. But everything depends upon whether the text cited is first hand evidence or not. No historian worthy of the name will be turned aside from such a document, for example, as the record of the Minutes of the fateful Austro-Hungarian Cabinet Meeting of July 7, 1914, to read the opinion on Austrian responsibility for the war of those who have never gone back to these prime sources to find out what happened.

As a matter of fact, the issue can be narrowed down to very simple terms. Everything falls into two categories, the more distant causes and those of the immediate outbreak. In the course of the controversy, the emphasis has shifted from one to the other according to its relative usefulness in proving a case. Historians have naturally had a tendency to emphasize the more remote causes. To explore the obscure and distant gives scholarship a pleasure which is not to be got from concentrating on things at hand. Thus the alleged "encirclement" of Germany by English diplomacy loomed large in the eyes of the Germans. But if the war had not broken out in 1914, no one could speak of the "encirclement" as a cause of war, simply because the war itself would not have happened. That this is not a quibble but a real fact to be kept in mind in judging the causes of the World War is clearly shown by other incidents when all the trend of history seemed pointing toward war and yet the conflict, avoided at a time of crisis, never came. The best example of this was the Fashoda crisis of 1898, when Kitchener in the Sudan forced an officer of France to haul down the tricolor. If England and France had gone to war on that occasion, as they almost did, the historian could have proven from at least two centuries of French and British rivalry in empire building, that such a war was unavoidable, owing to the imperialism of both countries. Instead of war came the first real friendship of both countries in all their history, the Entente Cordiale. This analogy is by no means sufficient to dispose of the distant causes of the World War in international rivalry, for they did set the stage for the alignment of the combatants; but they did not determine what the Austrian Government decided to do in 1914. The most telling proof that its decision was not necessarily forced upon it by past history is that Tisza, the Hungarian Prime Minister, was not for going to war — at least then. He was for diplomatic action which, if it had been taken, would certainly have changed Germany's position with reference to the Near East. In that case the question of Germany's responsibility for what might happen later would have been wholly different. It was what happened in 1914, not what happened in 1904, which caused the change from diplomacy to war.

Narrowing down the issue then to the immediate causes, everything leads in the last analysis to the meeting of the Austro-Hungarian cabinet and its relations with Parliament. At Vienna Berchthold was set upon having war with Serbia, for which the murder of the Archduke was hardly more than a pretext. Before the murder the Hapsburg Government had already been considering how to put Serbia in its place, finding it offensively aggressive after its recent successes in the Balkan wars. Tisza fought stubbornly for a cautious policy by way of diplomatic pressure, but Berchthold finally won him to his cause by reporting that Germany not only supported measures of force but was even impatient for action.

Everyone now agrees that Bethmann-Hollweg did not want war; nor for that matter did the Kaiser. But Berlin was in a difficult position; loyalty bound it to its ally, especially since Austrian existence depended so largely upon prestige [4] and that was presented as the supreme issue of the hour. There can be no doubt that Berchthold's boldness and duplicity dragged Germany further than it had any liking to go; nevertheless it followed the Austrian lead and this was taken by Russia to imply that Berlin was the real instigator of the war.

There are two kinds of responsibility, one for that kind of violent aggression which Hitler has used in Czechoslovakia and Poland, and the other an acquiescence in the acts of others. Although the degree of responsibility is much less in the latter case than in the former, the con-

[4] In the discussions of the Austrian Cabinet the word "prestige" is always to the fore as the chief issue.

sequences may be equally grave. It is true that at the very
last of the crisis Bethmann-Hollweg tried earnestly to hold
back his impetuous Austrian colleague, and that the German Kaiser was ready to accept the Serbian reply to the
Austrian ultimatum as a basis for a peaceful settlement.
But Vienna went on to bombard Belgrade and the German
Ambassador at St. Petersburg, insufficiently informed of
what the German Chancellor was trying to do, left Russia
under the mistaken impression that both governments were
equally set upon launching a European war.

There are all the elements of a Greek tragedy in this
situation, but the fact remains that Austria was chiefly
responsible for what followed, and that Germany, as its
partner, felt that it was in no position to risk that bold step
for peace which had to be taken if the war was to be
averted.

No student of these complicated happenings will be
satisfied with this short summary of those fateful days
which launched the World War. But these are central
facts which are not to be obscured by all the secondary detail in the war-guilt controversy. They are facts known
and accepted by all German scholars whose judgment is
worthy of attention. But they are not widely known or
given their true importance by a public which was never
called upon to weigh the evidence except for the purpose
of freeing Germany from the accusation of war guilt. The
fact that Russia began to mobilize before Germany, although not actually until Austria was marching on Belgrade, is so much more in the open than the complicated
story of negotiations, that the myth of Germany's relative
innocence is likely to persist; especially in a country in
which the youth is taught not history but doctrine.

Viewed in the light of History, both these terms of

"guilt" and "innocence" are, as Bethmann-Hollweg indicated, misleading. It is really a question of responsibility
rather than guilt; for prior to 1914, war was regarded as
a legitimate instrument of policy which could be used by
a sovereign state whenever its government deemed it necessary. Although throughout the centuries there had been
protests of moral and religious leaders against the use of
so cruel an instrument, nevertheless, the whole state structure of the politics of power rested upon the right to resort
to the arbitrament of arms. It was the World War itself
which carried into political statesmanship the moral issue
of war as an illegitimate thing in itself, an idea which has
rallied to its support the free opinion of democratic countries. The amount of latent support for it in Germany at
the present day is something that no one can possibly measure; but the German reaction against the charge of war
guilt seemed at first to be directed more towards pacifism
than militarism. The criticism which the Germans themselves made of the government of William II, had a moral
as well as a political implication. But then, as time passed,
the more thoughtful critics placed the moral blame upon
the pre-war state system itself; it was but a step from this
position to that of discounting any personal responsibilities,
or even that of any one government, on the theory that all
were involved in the same kind of political relationships.
Lloyd George has been widely quoted in support of this
theory; but his statement that Europe stumbled into the
war by a tragic set of blunders still leaves unsolved the
problem of apportioning responsibility, if not guilt; for
statesmen are responsible for their blunders as well as for
their conscious planning.

It is not likely that there can ever be full agreement on
this question of responsibility for the war of 1914; but

whatever disagreements persist, the controversy itself is a great gain to the peace movement. There was nothing like it when Drake "singed the beard of the Spanish King" in the harbor of Cadiz, or when Europe was laid waste by dynastic wars. The French Revolution, it is true, had a moral slogan to justify its crusade, and Bismarck knew the value of those "imponderables" which could be mobilized by diplomacy and journalism. But the World War marked the beginning of a revolution, not only in the art of warfare, but in the place of war in human society. Unfortunately for Germany, the concentration upon clearing itself from the attack of war guilt, geared into the issue of reparation, distorted its view of history and ultimately led to a reaffirmation of the politics of power in terms so crude that Bismarck, had he been living today, would have been the first to react against them.

CHAPTER VII

THE TREATY

It was not by chance that the so-called war guilt clause of the Treaty of Versailles (Article 231) was the introduction to the section on Reparation, for that was the section containing the most dubious exactions which Germany was obliged to accept, exactions extending into an indefinite future. Reparation involved continuing effort throughout years of peace to make good "the loss and damage" inflicted on the Allies in the war. No other part of the Treaty was so open to criticism as this which left the amount of reparation to be fixed by an Allied commission without any sure guarantee that Germany would be received back as a solvent nation for more than a generation. But here again as in the war guilt clause the Germans interpreted the clause at its worst. Stated in simplest terms, Germany was to pay an immediate sum equal to twenty billion gold marks for war damage and to give bonds for additional sums which would bring the whole amount to some sixty billion gold marks. Over and above this it was to pay an indefinite sum according to its capacity to pay.* The American delegation secured that this further amount should only be assessed by unanimous vote of the Reparation Commission and as at that time everyone in Paris expected that America would sign the Peace Treaty this meant that America would have a veto upon any further levies upon Germany. Had America signed the Treaty

---

* As a first installment, bonds for forty billion marks were to be issued when the Reparation Commission decided that Germany could service them.

there is no doubt that its veto would have held the Reparation payments down to the amount already agreed upon; because America as the chief creditor nation in the world would have had every reason for preventing new reparation claims upon the debtor Germany, since such an act would have lessened the value of America's holdings. By the refusal of the United States to sign the Treaty and its consequent withdrawal from Reparation negotiations except as an observer, it left Germany face to face with a situation in which France under Poincaré took the leadership. The disaster which that leadership brought to France and to Europe is too well known to need recital here.

Just how much Germany paid on reparation and other treaty accounts is a matter on which she and her creditors are in complete disagreement. For example, the German Government has maintained that, not counting what it paid under the Dawes and the Young plans, its payments totaled 56,577 million gold marks, of which 42,059 million were on reparation account, and 14,518 on the other exactions in the Treaty of Peace. Against this enormous sum the Reparation Commission's estimates reached only 10,426 million marks. In commenting on this, Messrs. Moulton and Pasvolsky, whose lucid summing up is followed here,[1] dismiss the problem with the following remark: [2] "This question is now only of historic interest since under the provisions of The Hague agreements, based on recommendations of the Young Plan, all outstanding unsettled accounts between Germany and the commission were declared closed. However, controversy

[1] Harold G. Moulton and Leo Pasvolsky, *War Debts and World Prosperity* (Washington, The Brookings Institution, 1932), pp. 260 ff. See also on the whole subject, Moulton and Maguire, *Germany's Capacity to Pay,* Chapter III and Appendices.
[2] *Op. cit.,* p. 261.

over the difference between the two official estimates still flares up occasionally." Unfortunately problems like this are not settled when they become "only of historic interest." The implication that history deals with a dead past and economics with a living present or future, was probably wholly unintentional but it corresponds with an error that persists in the minds of many. If ever there was a living fact, it was the wide-spread belief of the German people that their payments under the Treaty of Versailles were so vast as to dwarf every other cause of their economic difficulties in the post-war period.

As a matter of fact, the proportion of the difference between the estimate of the German Government and that of the Reparation Commission almost exactly parallels the difference between the financial costs of the war to the Government and the economic cost and displacement of the war. The larger sum includes such items as the labor of German prisoners of war, the cost of military and industrial disarmament, and a vastly greater figure than the Reparation Commission allowed on German property, public and private, that had been either ceded or confiscated. A complete analysis of these figures calls for a study on the nature of the continuing costs in the period of liquidation. This is ground that has already been fully traversed, however, and we may accept the conclusions of a competent and disinterested American calculation that the total amount paid by Germany was 21,585 million marks.[3] At the same time, it is perfectly clear to any student of this problem that the cost of Reparation to Germany was much more than the creditor nations received, through the disturbance in business and the difficulties of transfer; which is just what one ought to expect in liquidation and insolvency

[3] *Op. cit.*, p. 269.

proceedings. But even if we were to grant the larger sum that Germany claims as the extent of its "tribute money," it is only fair to deduct from it the enormous contribution of foreign investors, especially American, who, confident of Germany's capacity for economic recovery, sank their fortunes and their savings in the Reich. The estimate of the Dawes Report, that from 1919–1923 from seven to eight billion gold marks' worth of German (worthless) currency was sold abroad, is regarded by German experts as too high; but the deficit in Germany's balance of payments reached eleven billion gold marks in the four years 1919–1922, and this must have been mainly covered by the sale of marks through foreign speculators.[4] Thus, giving Germany the benefit of every doubt, the amount of Germany's payments under the Treaty is apparently about one quarter of what the War cost the nation. A more accurate balance sheet, however, would be that of the cost to the Government; here the statement commonly current in the allied countries stands: that foreign investors paid into Germany the equivalent of all it paid on reparation; which would leave the cost of the War as the one immeasurably heavy bill against Germany's finance.

It might seem that this would dispose of the whole problem. By no means. To deal only with the actual amounts paid leaves out of account the blighting influence of uncertainty until 1924 when the Dawes Plan finally set the standard annual obligation of Germany at 2.5 billion marks. The world of credit in which we live today needs certainty and confidence in the future and this was denied

[4] Costantino Bresciani-Turroni, *The Economics of Inflation*, p. 86. As to the income from Germany's pre-war foreign investments, these were in the neighborhood of twenty-five billion marks, of which, as we have seen above (p. 57), only about ten billion were left by the war to meet its debts abroad.

to Germany by the fact that the Reparation account was left open for so long. Although the final assessment was, as we see it now, much too high in view of the repercussion of the War upon world economy,[5] yet it is only fair to those who had to deal with this greatest of all liquidations, to note that in the years immediately following Germany seemingly enjoyed a temporary prosperity, and the rest of the world entered upon an even greater "boom." Looking back over this history, we should recall how completely at sea as to Germany's capacity to pay had been those who advised the Paris Peace Conference on Reparation. It was from such men as the Governor of the Bank of England, an office ordinarily filled by the most cautious of men, that the statement of Germany's ability to repair the losses of the War reached the highest "astronomical figures." One of the experts in the shaping of the reparations said to me at the time that he had had much experience in dealing with bankrupt firms, and that he had generally found that a bankrupt could pay about twice as much as at first seemed possible from an examination of his visible assets. It was not to be expected that the allied experts could know as much about Germany as its own economists and statesmen; and their argument that reparation and treaty costs were more than Germany could pay was based not upon any effort to find out what the long drawn out catastrophe had cost the Reich, but upon the business-man's method of day-to-day calculation based upon the trend of the market.

The practical method, moreover, of attempting to estimate Germany's "capacity to pay" on the basis of a going concern had two things in its favor: first, the costs of the War had been shared by the territories which were taken

[5] See Chapter VIII below.

from Germany in the Peace Treaty; and, second, the estimate of War costs constituted a problem in itself which
was no less difficult than that of estimating Germany's
post-war potentialities.

In the course of this discussion mention has been made
of other than Reparation payments in the Treaty settlement. Among these were those providing for the liquidation of the private property of German individuals in
enemy countries. The principle was adopted of giving
the Allies power to confiscate this private property. The
German Delegation did not wholly reject the principle
which underlay this exaction; they could not very well
do so in view of their own action in war time. The Allies
replied (June 17th) that during the war they had been
forced to take foreign investments from their citizens even
to the point of infringing on private rights and that now
the time had come when Germany must recognize their
right to treat her abroad with an equal disregard of the
effect upon private property.

Without doubt this looks like a step backward in international law, as it had become the rule in the development
of modern warfare that private property should be respected. But the World War was not only an industrial
revolution in warfare, it also marked the advent of what
might be called the socialization of warfare. Industries
and property were socialized in proportion as they could
contribute to the victory. We have seen above how the
"Hindenburg Program" socialized Germany in proportion as it militarized it. But the same process was true in
its enemy countries in greater or less degree. Consequently
the argument over the illegality of the seizure of private
property could not be pressed to the point of insisting upon
its total immunity. On the other hand, the Treaty opened

the doors too widely so that in some countries it resulted in practically total confiscation. The impartial historian will probably have to draw the line somewhere between both extremes; but again as in the case of Reparation the post-war policies were fully as much to blame as the Treaty.

The other economic clauses that dealt with commercial relations were, at least in theory, much more liberal than those which Germany had planned in wartime for its own future; indeed they were largely designed to prevent the revival of anything like that Middle European customs union which Germany and Austria had negotiated during the war. The liberalizing principle which was adopted was that Germany should grant "most favored nation treatment" for five years to the Allied Powers, an arrangement which called for the adjustment of various commercial treaties. There was nothing in this Provision which would work out to Germany's disadvantage if the other signatories were to pursue liberal trade policies. Unfortunately the United States, fearing that the hard-pressed nations of Europe would attempt to recover prosperity by dumping their goods on the American market, was a prime leader away from the policy of lowered tariffs; and the newly formed states of Central Europe gave expression to continuing animosities by erecting tariff barriers on a dozen new frontiers. The Treaty itself played almost no part in the erection of these impediments to trade from which other industrial countries as well as Germany suffered in the post-war period, beyond the fact that it had sanctioned the creation of more sovereignties than had existed in the pre-war period. Here again we are dealing chiefly with post-war history.

Another group of economic problems centered around

the control of ports, waterways and railways. A genuine international control was provided on the foundations that had been laid down at the Congress of Vienna in 1815. In order, however, to provide access to the sea for land-locked countries like Switzerland and Czechoslovakia, German rivers like the Rhine, Oder and Elbe were put under the control of international commissions on which Germany was in the minority. The conditions of rail transport were subsequently defined by an International Transport Conference which the League of Nations held at Barcelona in 1921; and the actual conditions of railway traffic as evolved in the ensuing years under the joint pressures of politics and business gave Germany workable arrangements.

Whatever we think of the financial and economic clauses of the Treaty of Versailles, by the end of the first decade after the war, in 1928, Germany was apparently relatively about as well off as its former enemies. This was not wholly evident in the false prosperity of the Twenties. But when the boom burst it was seen that the country which had apparently come most successfully through the war and its liquidation, the United States, was the one which had strained its credit most seriously and suffered the most disastrous results therefrom. The chief creditor nation lost most in the collapse of credit. It is true that if Germany had been forced to meet all its private as well as public debts abroad it would have collapsed under the strain but the policy of "fulfilment" kept the door open for adjustment and finally for cancellation. This point is all-important in judging the claim of Hitler that he saved Germany from its economic servitudes. The fact is that it was saved from those servitudes before Hitler came to power. One wonders how long it will be before the German people do justice to both their own republican statesmanship and the democratic trend of public opinion in the ex-enemy countries which found voice in Briand and Herriot, MacDonald and Austen Chamberlain and Herbert Hoover.

More serious because more difficult to change were the territorial clauses of the Treaty of Versailles. Of these, the cession to France of Alsace and Lorraine created no problem because Germany had definitely accepted their return to France in the Armistice negotiations. Similarly, the return of Northern Schleswig to Denmark by plebiscite had been promised Denmark by Bismarck in the Peace of Nikolsburg in 1866. The Saar Valley was placed for fifteen years under a commission of the League of Nations but with a plebiscite which brought it back to Germany in 1935. Its coal mines were ceded to France because of the wanton destruction, contrary to the rules of war, of the mines in northern France. Thus with the exception of the three little frontier districts acquired by Belgium, the western and northern frontiers were rectified in ways that had historical justification.

This leaves only one vital issue for Germany in the territorial settlement: the eastern frontier. Germany had agreed to the restoration of Poland with a guarantee of free access to the sea. This narrowed the issue down to two questions: what was Poland and how was it to have a window on the Baltic? In both of these, the Paris Peace Conference tried to give Poland frontiers that would protect it against becoming a mere dependency of Germany. It would have been a cynical and lying gesture to have proclaimed the restoration of Poland and yet to have left Germany in a position to make Polish sovereignty a snare and a delusion. The pre-war frontiers of Germany on the east, although they had stood for over a hundred years, had never registered justice but had set the seal upon the partitions of Polish territory and left in German hands the richest, if not the largest, share of that vast booty which fell to the robber monarchies when they extinguished Polish freedom. Long possession, however, had made the Germans feel that the fringe of Poland which they had taken was their own land by unquestioned right. On the other hand, the technical experts who advised President Wilson used German maps to show how wholly Polish were areas of this border region of Germany and the historians could support the geographers by showing how even Bismarck had failed to solve "the Polish question," beaten by the persistent movement of population.

These are but a few of the facts which confronted the makers of the Treaty of Versailles as they grappled with the problem of putting back into the map of Europe a country which had not been there for almost as long a period as that of the whole history of the United States. Clearly no settlement could be made without heavy sacrifices on the part of Germany, and if the frontier were to follow ethnographic lines and to reach as well to a port on the Baltic, there was something to be said for the Treaty — even including Upper Silesia.[6] There were those at Paris, more especially in the British Delegation, who contended that to push a Corridor across Prussia would result in accentuating nationalism and prevent the working out of a real guarantee for Polish security which could only be developed through friendly relations with Germany.

---

[6] The Treaty left the settlement of Upper Silesia to a plebiscite which was duly held, and if the frontier that followed upon it was unjustly drawn, as the Germans claimed, the fault lay with post-war statesmen and not with the Treaty of Versailles.

They pointed out that Danzig, while a German city, had always been the seaport for Polish trade and that mutual economic advantage would be the best safeguard for Poland's future. It is by no means sure that if their advice had been followed the reactionary Junker of East Prussia would have understood any such enlightened statesmanship, or that German opinion generally, so long accustomed to looking down upon the Poles as an inferior people, would have been ready to deal with them on even terms under a juster peace. But the fact remains that the Junkers and the German nationalists were given grounds for their antagonism to which they could rally the liberal if none-too-well-informed opinion in other countries against the whole Treaty. This strange alliance pleaded the cause of Germany against the Treaty with unremitting zeal, until it would seem as if most people everywhere except the non-Germanic nations on the Continent of Europe thought of the Treaty of Versailles as though it were a vast conspiracy against the very life and liberties of the German people; whereas the "unendurable servitudes" were only those in the sections on Reparation and the Polish settlement.

This conclusion, however, leaves frankly out of account two other sections of the Treaty against which Germany protests with equal vigor, those on the colonies and on armaments. It is a deep-seated conviction of Nazi Germany that the recovery of the colonies is necessary for its economic life; yet Germany's trade with its colonies in 1913 was less than one-half of one per cent of its total foreign trade. The colonies were yielding little, and their yield could not be materially increased without a vastly larger capital outlay than post-war Germany could have put into them. As for their supplying the raw materials which

Germany needed, it might at least occur to some of the most vehement opponents of that section of the Treaty that one can get raw materials only where they exist and that Germany's colonies lacked most of its essential needs. Moreover, those Germans who have waged the strongest battle for the return of the colonies have done so on the theory that they should become closed preserves for Germany itself and be treated as tributary sources of supply mainly for military purposes. That the choice lay between that kind of an extension of military economics over the seven seas and a mandate system set up by the Treaty of Versailles is too often forgotten by those who would tear up the provisions of the Versailles Treaty in this regard.

As for the disarmament of Germany provided for in the Treaty, the principle upon which it was based was set forth in the preamble to Part V, that it was to enable the other powers to disarm similarly. Had they done so, all the world would have shared the economic benefits which this section conferred upon Germany by lessening to the dimensions of a police force the cost of military and naval establishments. Again as in every other section with which we have been dealing, it was the post-war policies which were to blame for not realizing the implied promise of the terms of peace. As it was, Germany and its allies were alone reduced to impotence, and this in a matter which struck most deeply at the pride and even the self-respect of the German people. It is hard for any foreigner to appreciate how much of the national pride of Germany was centered in its army. We have touched upon this before, but it cannot be too strongly emphasized that the army stood for more than safety; it was the one institution which in German eyes was still the symbol of glorious triumph at a time when everything else was submerged in the atmosphere of defeat. To single it out for destruction and still to leave other armies on the soil of Europe was sure to bring back that spirit of militarism against which German democracy had reacted in vain in the pre-war years. But when we judge adversely, as we must, the failure of the Disarmament conferences, we come upon the fact that, with all of its idealism as exhibited in the Washington Naval Disarmament Conference, the United States was itself one of the chief impediments to genuine disarmament; because for a whole decade after the War it refused to help to put anything in the place of war, by its denial of the League of Nations and the World Court. War remains an instrument of policy to which nations will resort in spite of the Paris Peace Pact or any other such pronouncement so long as no other provision is made by international agreement for dealing with those fundamental differences upon which nations divide. History has shown that diplomacy is not enough, and it has also shown that a league of nations is inadequate so long as any great power withholds its coöperation from the forces that make for peace and allows its resources to reach the aggressor as well as the victim. In short, the problem of disarmament is a problem of world order and law, not merely of military technique; upon this basis history will judge the relative responsibilities of those who weakened or thwarted the efforts of the League of Nations, as well as the failure of those efforts in themselves. The nations outside the League have no alibi when it comes to placing the blame for what happened in keeping alive militarism in a world which both morally and economically was hopefully trying to escape from it.

In this short sketch of a vast field of history, generalizations have been stated which should be followed up by the detailed study of every phase of recent history, not only that of Germany but of the whole post-war world. The need for such study is urgent and compelling if the peace which must follow the present war is to avoid the blunders of the last. For no treaty, no proclamation of principles, will save civilization from disaster if the nations themselves refuse to learn the fundamental lesson that the era of applied science is one of increasing interdependence, as time and space are mastered by invention, and that the old sovereignties must cease to be the instruments of anarchy. There are various kinds of anarchy: the violent and aggressive type which Hitler personifies, and the non-coöperative, isolationist type which is the unconscious accomplice of the militarist. These facts, unwelcome as some of them are, furnish the only sound basis for judging the policies of nations both now and in the future.

It would be a happy clarification of all our difficulties if at this point we could add up the total cost of the Treaty of Versailles to Germany or describe its effects upon German economy in somewhat the same way we have dealt with the costs of the War. And at first sight it would seem to be a much easier and simpler problem. Definite payments were made and definite resources subtracted from Germany's pre-war wealth. But apart from the amount paid in Reparation, in which, as we have seen, there was also room for disagreement, the measurement of the value of the ceded property and territories opens the door to utter disagreement. What, for instance, was the value of the German Colonies? In terms of past history, they were worth little; in fact, they were a liability rather than an asset. But in terms of future development, the Germany of today claims that they have great possibilities. Even more difficult is the estimate of the value of the part of Upper Silesia which was taken by Poland, for the boundary line cuts across an industrial territory in a way that opens the door to the most diverse evaluations. Then, too, should one add in Alsace Lorraine which Germany readily agreed to give back to France? If it is to be included, should it be assessed on the basis of all its natural resources or only on the developments under the German regime? In either case, a most difficult if not impossible problem.

Even if we could make an accurate statement of these losses, it would now be of little more than academic value because they were summed up once and for all so far as German public opinion was concerned by the German delegation at Versailles in its protest against the economic clauses of the Treaty. After referring to the fact that Germany as an industrial state was obliged to import foodstuffs to keep her population alive and that the Treaty rendered this difficult by the loss of German shipping and colonies, the document summarizes in the following terms the economic effect of the cession of territory: [7]

By the putting into force of the Territorial Clauses of the Treaty of Peace, Germany would lose to the East the most important regions for the production of corn and potatoes, which would be equivalent to the loss of 21 per cent. of the total crop of those articles of food. Moreover, the intensity of our agricultural production would diminish considerably. On the one hand, the importation of certain raw material indispensable for the production of manure, such as phosphates, would be hindered; on the other hand, this industry would suffer like all other industries from lack of coal. The Treaty of Peace provides for the loss of almost a third of the production of our coal mines. Apart from this decrease, we are forced for ten

[7] The chairman of the Economic Commission of the German delegation who drafted this statement was Dr. Carl Melchior, who in 1922 became chairman of the German editorial board for the *Economic and Social History of the World War* referred to in the next chapter.

years to deliver enormous consignments of coal to various
Allied countries.

Moreover, in conformity with the Treaty, Germany will
concede to her neighbors nearly three-quarters of her mineral
production, and more than three-fifths of her zinc production.

After this diminution of her products, after the economic
depression caused by the loss of her Colonies, of her merchant
fleet, and of her possessions abroad, Germany would not be in
a state to import from abroad a sufficient quantity of raw material. An enormous part of German industry would therefore
inevitably be condemned to destruction. At the same time,
the necessity of importing foodstuffs would increase considerably, whilst the possibility of satisfying that demand would
diminish in the same proportion.

This passage, although but a single extract from one of
the documents, gives some idea of the strength of the
attack upon the Treaty by the German delegation at Versailles. It is not possible here to follow the issue through
in detail; but the reader will want to know what the Allied
and Associated Powers had to say in rebuttal. The pertinent
sections of the letter of Clemenceau of May 22, 1919, ran
as follows:

4. Great stress is laid upon the proposal that on the Eastern
side Germany shall be deprived of the regions specially devoted
to the production of wheat and potatoes. This is true. But
the Note fails altogether to observe that there is nothing in
the Peace Treaty to prevent either the continued production
of these commodities in the areas in question, or their importation into Germany. On the contrary, the free admission of the
products of the Eastern districts is provided for during a period
of three years. Moreover, it is fortunate for Germany that
these regions have lost none of their productivity owing to the
ravages of war. They have escaped the shocking fate which

was dealt out by the German armies to the corresponding
territories in Belgium and France on the West, and Poland,
Russia, Roumania and Serbia on the East. There appears to be
no reason why their produce should not continue to find a
market on German soil.

5. Stress is laid upon the proposed restriction of the import
of phosphates. It is, however, forgotten that Germany has
never produced but has always imported the phosphates of
which she stands in need. Nor is there anything in the Terms
of Peace which will prevent or hinder the importation of phosphates into Germany in the future. Other countries, which do
not produce phosphates, are also compelled to import them in
common with many other products from the outside; and the
only difference in the two situations will arise from the relative
degree of wealth or impoverishment in the countries concerned.

6. The German Note makes special complaint of the dep-
rivation of coal, and asserts that nearly one-third of the production of the existing coal mines will be lost. But it omits to
notice that one-fourth of the pre-war consumption of German
coal was in the territories which it is now proposed to transfer.
Further it fails to take into account the production of lignite,
eighty million tons of which were produced annually in Germany before the war, and none of which is derived from the
transferred territories. Neither is any reference made to the
fact that the output of coal in the non-transferred districts was
rapidly increasing before the war, and that there is no reason
to doubt that under proper management there will be a continuing increase in the future.

7. But should not the coal situation be viewed from a different and wider standpoint? It cannot be forgotten that among
the most wanton acts of devastation perpetrated by the German armies during the war was the almost complete destruction
by her of the coal supplies of Northern France. An entire
industry was obliterated with a calculation and a savagery
which it will take many years to repair. The result has been

a grave and prolonged shortage of coal in Western Europe. There can be no reason in equity why the effect of this shortage should be borne exclusively by the Allied nations who were its victims, or why Germany, who deliberately made herself responsible for the deficiency, should not, to the full limit of her capacity, make it good.

8. Stress is also laid upon the hardships alleged to be inflicted upon Germany by the necessity of importing in future iron ores and zinc. It is not understood why Germany should be supposed to suffer from conditions to which other countries contentedly submit. It would appear to be a fundamental fallacy that the political control of a country is essential in order to procure a reasonable share of its products. Such a proposal finds no foundation in economic law or in history.

9. The Allied and Associated Powers cannot accept the speculative estimate presented to them in the German Note on the future conditions of German industry as a whole. This estimate appears to them to be characterized and vitiated by palpable exaggerations. No note is taken of the fact that the economic disaster produced by the war is wide-spread, and, indeed, universal. Every country is called upon to suffer. There is no reason why Germany, which was responsible for the war, should not suffer also.

Thus Clemenceau brings to the fore two factors in the light of which the Treaty must be judged: the war, not yet a thing of the past, whose universal devastation had somehow or other to be restored; and the hope for coöperative policies of the future which would make the "servitudes" of the Treaty so much less than they seemed to be when regarded in the light of war economy. The post-war years, however, were to obscure the one and deny the other. And again we come back to the fact that not the least of the policies which made the settlement worse than even war-torn nations demanded was the withdrawal of America from the League of Nations, weakening and denaturing the one instrument for peaceful change which Wilson had counted upon to make the Treaty ultimately just.

A week later, on May 29, 1919, the German Delegation submitted its final document, the Counter Proposals, on the "Conditions of Peace." This was in the form of a series of detailed memoranda prepared by the various experts on the different questions covered by the Treaty, a study of which is necessary for anyone who wishes to reach an impartial judgment on the terms of the settlement. We must limit ourselves here, however, to the few pertinent paragraphs of the covering letter which summarizes in nontechnical language the chief points upon which Germany was then ready to coöperate:

Germany knows that she must consent to sacrifices, in order to obtain peace. She knows that, in conformity with a convention, she has promised these sacrifices; she is ready to go to the extreme limit of what is possible.

1. Germany offers to anticipate all other nations, by her own disarmament, to show that she wants to help create the new era of Peace of Right. She sacrifices obligatory military service and reduces her army to 100,000 men, abstraction being made for transitory measures. She even renounces the warships that her enemies still wish to leave to her. But it is taken for granted, that she will be immediately admitted with the same right as the other states, into the League of Nations and that a true League of Nations will be formed, including all the Nations, admitted by good will, even the enemies of to-day. This League will have the sentiment of responsibility before Humanity, as foundation, and will have a power of coercion, sufficiently strong and worthy of confidence, to protect the frontiers of its members.

2. As far as territorial questions are concerned, Germany places herself, without reservation, on the ground of Wilson's

program. She renounces her rights of sovereignty over Alsace-Lorraine, but desires a free plebiscite. She gives to Poland the greater part of Posnania, the territories indisputably inhabited by Poles and the capital of Posen. She is ready to insure to the Poles by the cession of free ports at Danzig, Koenigsberg and Memel, by a chart governing navigation on the Vistula and by special treaties regarding railways, free and certain access to the sea without international guarantees. Germany is ready to insure the economic supply of France in coal, especially from the Saar coal field, until restoration of the French mines. The parts of Schleswig which have a Danish majority will be given to Denmark after a plebiscite. Germany requests that the right of self-determination be also respected in favor of the Germans of Austria and Bohemia.

She is ready to put all her colonies under the administration in common of the League of Nations, if she is recognized as mandatory for the latter.

3. Germany is ready to make the payments incumbent upon her according to the peace program agreed upon, up to the maximum sum of 100 billion marks gold, of which 20 billion marks gold are to be paid by May 1, 1926, the other 80 billion marks gold in annual sums without interest. These sums are in principle to represent a percentage fixed according to the revenue of the Empire and the German States. The quota will approach the former budget of peace times. For the first ten years, it shall not exceed a billion marks gold. The German taxpayer shall not be taxed less than the most highly taxed taxpayer among those represented on the Commission of Reparations.

Germany supposes from this that she will not have to make other territorial sacrifices than those heretofore cited, and that she will be permitted all liberty of movement at home and abroad.

4. Germany is ready to put all her economic force at the service of reconstruction. She desires to collaborate by her work in the reconstruction of the ravaged districts of Belgium

and the North of France. For the deficit in the production of the mines destroyed in the North of France she will furnish as high as 20 million tons of coal for the first five years, 8 million tons a year for the next five years. Germany will facilitate other deliveries of coal to France, Belgium, Italy and Luxembourg.

Moreover, Germany is ready to furnish important quantities of benzol, coal tar, sulphuric ammonia and dye-stuffs and pharmaceutical products.

5. Finally, Germany offers to put her entire merchant tonnage at the disposal of the world's commerce, to put at the disposal of the enemy a part of the cargoes, which shall be put to her credit toward the damages to be repaired, and for a term of years to construct for them in German yards a tonnage whose figure exceeds their demands.

6. To replace the river boats destroyed in Belgium and the North of France, Germany offers her own river fleet.

7. Germany thinks that she sees an appropriate means of rapidly fulfilling her obligations in the way of reparation, by according industrial participation, especially in the coal mines, to insure the delivery of coal.

No fair-minded reader of these few paragraphs can fail to ask how much of Germany's grievance against the Treaty of Versailles lay in the substance of its exactions and how much in the manner in which they were imposed. The German people, bewildered by defeat that had belied their military expectations and exhausted physically and spiritually by hardship and disaster, were now called upon to face a humiliation which struck fully as deep into their moral life as the material losses seemed to threaten their chance of economic recovery. But here again the continuing cost of the War played its sinister part. The very people to whom integrity meant most, those whose savings had been lost and who were being forced into a new proletariat, were torn between the maintenance of democratic ideals and the alluring but specious appeal of national socialism. In this confused state of mind the party of action offered them a program, vague and ill thought through so far as its positive doctrine went, but vehement in its attack upon the continuing symbol of Germany's humiliation, the Treaty of Versailles.

CHAPTER VIII

THE COSTS OF THE WORLD WAR

We do not know, and can never know, the full costs of of the World War; or of any war. The history of post-war Germany sketched in this short study leads to no other conclusion. Yet, while exact figures can never be given, because war never excludes the continuing activities of peace, and the two economies are inextricably interlocked, nevertheless, if figures are taken as descriptive rather than absolute measurements, it is possible even to draw comparisons between costs of war and of the other elements in a national economy.

It is in this sense that we have ventured, in the course of this study, to indicate how much of Germany's post-war burden was a result of the war and how much, comparatively, was due to what it paid on Reparation and Treaty accounts. The former was about four times as much as the latter. This is equally true, whether we are speaking of the relative financial costs to the Government of the Reich, or of the relative economic costs to the German people.

Another set of comparisons, equally open to criticism in detail, but more valid as a basis of judgment on the problem as a whole, is to be found in a comparison of the estimate of the war costs of other countries. The only comprehensive effort to cover this whole field was that of the *Economic and Social History of the World War*, published under the auspices of the Carnegie Endowment for International Peace, for which I have had the responsibility of direction and editorship.[1] Its one hundred and fifty volumes penetrated deeply into various aspects of war economy, but it is upon the whole more descriptive than statistical, and the final summing up of war costs is approached with great caution in each national series of studies. However, some light is thrown upon our problem of the relative costs of the war to Germany by such data as the following.

Mr. Francis W. Hirst, who drew up the balance sheets of war costs to Great Britain,[2] did not attempt to draw together into one single total the various elements of cost in losses in killed and wounded, in unemployment, in diminished trade, and the financial register of economic loss in taxation and debt. Any one familiar with the British method of presenting financial statistics knows that they differ from the American method in that they prefer to present wealth in terms of income rather than of capital sums. It is undoubtedly a more accurate method but it leaves the American reader with a less real sense of the magnitude of figures such as those involved in stating the economic effect of a World War. On the other hand, the statement that the Government spent some ten billion pounds sterling (six billion in pre-war values) on the War itself means less to an Englishman than that his taxes were raised to a point that almost threatened confiscation of the property of the well-to-do. For example, in 1921–1922 the national expenditure of Great Britain was £26. 2s. 6d. per head, while the French Government was spending £16, and the German Reich, including the States, only about

---

[1] Published in America by the Yale University Press.
[2] *The Consequences of the War to Great Britain.*

£4. 8s. per head. These figures, of course, represent the total costs of government in the different countries, not the War costs only; but they show the relative weight of the burden that the people in each country were bearing at a time when they were seeking to clear away the aftermath of the War. The English taxation was then about four times as heavy as that of Germany. At the same time the capital burden of the British national debt, which rose during the war from £650 million in 1914 to £7,435 million in 1919, remained with very little net reduction until 1933, although the interest rate was lowered by various transactions, into the details of which it is impossible to enter here. Thus with its enormously heavy burden of taxation the deficit of the British Treasury, most of which was undoubtedly traceable to the War and its continuing impact upon the economy of Great Britain, was close to the capital sum of 35 billion dollars.[3]

Professor Charles Gide, the dean of French economists and the chairman of the French Editorial Board, was very cautious in summing up the effect of the War upon France, especially in view of the lax methods of bookkeeping described by Professors Jeze and Truchy in their volume, *The War Finance of France*, but starting from a base of one hundred and eighty billion francs "as a legacy of the War," — a total worked out from the calculation of the Economic Conference of Brussels in 1920 — he comes to the following conclusion: that if an inventory had been taken of the fortune of France in the shape of its private fortunes, only about half of it would have been left at the end of the War.[4] The natural resources of France were, of course, still there, but their human ownership

[3] See Hirst, *op. cit.*, Book II, Chapter 2.
[4] Gide and Oualid, *Le Bilan de la Guerre pour la France*, p. 77.

and capacity for economic development had lessened by this amount. As he points out, however, this method of describing the impact of the War must not be taken as an unqualified historical statement of what happened. It is valid as indicating the measure of the effort which would have to be made to reconstruct a ruined world.

The most difficult of all war costs to estimate is naturally that of the late Austro-Hungarian Monarchy. Fortunately, however, Vienna, the former home of a great school of economists, was not unequal to the task. Under Professor Friedrich Wieser, the Austro-Hungarian Editorial Board prepared a program for a most elaborate series of analyses, the completion of which was in part frustrated by Professor Wieser's death. Recently, however, at my request, Professor Wilhelm Winkler, the distinguished statistician who had worked with Professor Wieser, went over his material again, the most puzzling and confusing for a statistician to deal with, — and drew up a statement of the results of his calculations which are being published as a supplement to the *Economic and Social History of the World War*. He has stated his conclusions in various ways, but they were summarized by him in a single sentence. In Austria-Hungary, — "the costs of the war were about five times as great as the annual national income, and almost four fifths as great as Austria-Hungary's national wealth."

The estimate of the cost of the war to the United States made by Professor John Maurice Clark,[5] one of the most penetrating studies in the whole series, was unfortunately written before the Depression and while a settlement of war debts was still a matter to be reckoned with. The tidal

[5] *The Cost of the World War to the People of the United States.* (1931.)

flood of liquidation which began in 1929 destroyed the bases of all previous calculations; at the same time it made impossible the formulation in anything approaching exact figures of the cost of the war to the United States. We shall see this later as we view the economic history of the period in general terms; but, as we have already seen above, the mere listing of astronomical totals is all but meaningless even for those who deal in world finance. A realistic picture of what happened can be got only by turning from national economics as a whole to the individual lives of the people themselves. It would be an illuminating thing to have a series of studies showing how the continuing influences of the World War affected the lives and fortunes of the average man, the farmer, the storekeeper, the owners of small industries and those living from limited incomes, bankers of moderate wealth and day laborers with little or no savings. When we think of the impact of war upon a national economy, what we really mean is the way in which it cuts in upon the lives of men and women such as these.

While it would carry us too far afield to explore the effect of the World War upon all these varied sections of the nation, we can form some idea of its extent by following the fortunes of that part of the population which would seem at first sight to have been least affected by the war, the farmers of a purely agricultural State like Iowa. By industry and thrift, this population, drawn mostly from old-world immigrants, had gained a much prized decent economic independence. Their farms were their own; debt was a thing to be avoided; and speculation almost a sin. With the World War the price of wheat went up to a dollar a bushel and beyond, and farmlands suddenly became worth five, ten or twenty times as much as they had been before. "Boom times" burst upon the prairies and the farmers began to speculate, borrowing money to buy more land. The worst of this process came not during the war itself but in the post-war years when syndicates opened up vast stretches of the land which never should have been plowed, the dry lands which were to become the "dust bowl" of America. Then came the crash and the over-taxed credit of the agricultural States was drained to support the overtaxed credit of Wall Street banks and insurance companies. The farmers, unable to meet their payments, lost their farms, or would have done so if the Government and the financial interests themselves had not helped to save something from the wreck. Similar liquidation faced industry and, indeed, the savings of the whole nation. Thus the American people was called upon, from 1929 to the present, in the last economic battle of the World War, to hold the defences of American civilization, — home, school, and the opportunity for living — against the threat of universal anarchy.

This far did the blow which the Austrian Government — relying on the aid of Germany, — aimed at distant Serbia, reach out across the world to ruin the hopes of people so remote that they had almost no knowledge at all of the origin of the conflict. In tracing the effect of the war into the heart of the middle western States, however, it may seem as though we had left the theme of this study far behind, that of the effect of the war upon Germany. As a matter of fact, the fundamental conclusion to be drawn from this short survey is that the World War revealed, as nothing else had ever done before, the interdependence of the nations of the modern world. The cost of the War to Germany cannot be considered apart from what it cost other peoples, neutrals as well as belligerents. It must be measured not only in terms of the loss or disturbance in its own productive industries but also in terms of the loss or disturbance to its customers, those with whom it was carrying on business abroad to the extent of some twenty-one billion marks in 1913. German industry, proportionately even more than that of the United States, was geared to a world market. It was therefore of the first importance for Germany that it should explore how world trade could be revived. This the Weimar Republic, with all its handicaps, was prepared to do; but Nazi Germany turned its face in the opposite direction. With a proud gesture, it shut itself off from the effort to break down barriers to trade by reciprocal or coöperative policies; the trend so perseveringly pursued by Secretary Hull. The United States had had rather more than its share of responsibility for the erection of these barriers in the post-war years; but when it called for a reconsideration of past policies, Nazi Germany was launched upon another career, that of autarky. This, as we shall see, was the final form in which World War costs came home to Germany.

The story is familiar to all, though the significance of it has not been fully seen. The liquidation of the Treaty, upon which the Nazi concentrated, and which was the occasion for so much rejoicing in Germany, was carried out in a way which blocked the liquidation of the remaining economic and financial disturbances arising out of the World War. The political reasons for this are easy to understand. The spectacle of other nations writing off their losses in the early Thirties, — when the very citadels of world finance, dollar, pound and franc, were partly washed away in the rising tide of apparent national insolvency, — was one to terrify all Germans who had lost their property in the great inflation of 1923. It is doubtful if any government of the Reich could have survived if it had allowed German money to follow the dollar and pound. The memory of past sufferings was too keen for that. But the result of Germany's refusal to allow its currency to submit to the normal play of economic forces was that it entered upon a state of financial and commercial siege. This is more than a figure of speech. For we must not blind ourselves to the fact that autarchy [6] is an organization of the State copied from military models, and that its ultimate justification, apart from such satisfaction as it gives to a submissive population at home, lies in its ability to force its will upon other peoples, — which is the definition of war in the military manuals from the day of Clausewitz.

The penalty for militarism is more militarism, with increased risk of war. We have seen this in the armament race; it is equally true in economic warfare. In Germany these two — rearmament and autarky — went hand in hand, with consequences fateful for all the world.

It has been asserted on Germany's behalf, and the text above might seem to bear it out, that Dr. Schacht, the strategist of autarky, had no other alternative, if Germany was to be held back from the brink of another inflation. It is true that Germany's creditors, including the United States, were unwilling to compromise and lessen their claims, pocketing their loss in the interest of world prosperity. But the reason for this intransigeance was that the German autarchy was rapidly becoming a great war machine and the chief demands were for military supplies. It is, of course, impossible to say what the other Powers would have done to aid a peaceful Germany; but, even as

---

[6] It might be worth while remarking that here as elsewhere in the volume, "autarchy" is used for political, "autarky" for economic independence.

it was, there were hopeful feelers sent out, especially in 1936, after the tripartite currency agreement which has so beneficially steadied exchanges between France, England and the United States. In November of that year, the International Chamber of Commerce acting with the Carnegie Endowment for International Peace, prepared a list of suggestions for removing barriers to trade, which had strong unofficial support; but, although German collaborators worked on it, the document was barred from Germany because of an incidental remark in it to the effect that colonies and raw materials were two separate questions to be dealt with each on its own ground. Two weeks before, Hitler at Nuremberg had said that they were one question. The whole proposal was therefore completely ignored. Without wishing to make more out of this incident than lies on the face of it, one is forced to the conclusion that the militarized State creates its own difficulties in dealing with peaceful nations.

To pursue this subject farther would carry us afield. But we have surveyed the post-war history of Germany enough to reach certain conclusions. We have seen that Germany, while it liquidated the Treaty, has only postponed its final liquidation of the War. The economy of autarky by which it has defended the mark in the world's currencies may have been forced upon it at home by the fact that no government could face another inflation and survive. But some government of Germany will have to liquidate the War before the accounts are finally cleared; for the illusion, or delusion, under which Germany fights its economic battles today, that it can force the rest of the world to its economic terms, is a left-over of the economy of war, and war economics do not make for ultimate prosperity. In short, Germany's attempt to escape from the continuing economic disturbances due to the War can only succeed if it can enslave the rest of the world in the same kind of economic fetters as it wears today.

This is clearly set forth — though naturally not in these terms — by Herr Hitler in his New Year Proclamation for 1940. His autarchy is to be a model for all Europe and will be imposed upon it by the might of German arms:

We fight, therefore, not only against the injustice of Versailles but to prevent the even greater injustice intended to replace it. We are fighting for the construction of a new Europe.

The "even greater injustice" is the continued existence of international finance in the hands, of course, of "Jewish reactionary warmongers in the capitalistic democracies." In such terms does the Führer wage war on the world of business as it is organized today, that of free enterprise and competitive capitalism. In its stead, he says:

As distinguished from Herr Chamberlain, we are convinced that a new Europe can be established not from the aged forces of a crumbling world or by the so-called statesmen who are not even able to solve the simplest problems in their own countries, but that the construction of a new Europe belongs to those people and forces which, on the basis of their attitude and accomplishments thus far, can be described as young and productive.

The Berlin correspondent of the New York *Times* reported how these war aims of Hitler were amplified at great length by innumerable inspired articles in the German press representing the present war as "a great 'international revolution' destined to make an end both to capitalistic society and the Western idea of national [sovereign] State in favor of the 'socialistic millennium,' which is to usher in the socialistic planning not only within nations but also among nations."

To this challenge — which parallels the utmost claims of the red international — the answer is the same as that which the democracies have made to communism. "Your aims may be high, your aspiration for social justice a noble one; but you pursue it both at home and abroad by the denial of every form of justice to those whose interest or even whose thoughts are opposed to your own."

The masters of Nazi Germany, thinking to liquidate the Treaty of Versailles, have thrown Europe back into the maelstrom of war costs from which it has been struggling to escape ever since 1919. The process that makes for universal bankruptcy is even more threatening now than when the Treaty of Versailles attempted, with such ill success, to canalize it in Reparation. There is no hope that Germany can now turn that process back upon its enemies and wreak revenge. The result which Hitler hopes for in this proclamation, that of a socialistic millennium, can no more be realized by the disasters of war than an increase in prosperity was possible to those who suffered the consequences of 1914.

CHAPTER IX

TRACING THE CONSEQUENCES

To trace the economic consequences of the World War beyond the few indications presented here would call for a synthesis built of much more varied material than is offered in this short summary. The analysis has in great measure been made in the *Economic and Social History of the World War*, which also, as we have seen, contains some important essays in synthesis. But the fact remains that economists have, until very recently, been strangely indifferent to the greatest single economic fact in modern history, that of the mobilization of all the civilized world upon a single objective — War.[1] The explanations of this

[1] In this connection it may not be out of place to quote the two opening paragraphs of *Crisis Government* by Professor Lindsay Rogers (New York, 1934):

Just before the change of administration in Washington on March 4, 1933, there were published two massive volumes — *Recent Social Trends* — which, with supporting monographs, had been prepared at a cost of half a million dollars under the direction of a commission appointed by Herbert Hoover. In these volumes tendencies and trends are dealt with for the most part as if they had not been accelerated or retarded by a war which from 1914 to 1918 rocked the world and left a legacy of peace treaties — or, in other words, a legacy of seeds of another war.

Only the writers of the "Trends" section on economic organization appeared to think that the War was of any importance. They properly believed that the conflict "has been a dominant influence on the economic life of the United States since 1914"; but elsewhere in the volume the War is mentioned only in speculation whether post-war periods mean an increase or decrease of the criminal laws that legislatures pass and in showing the always rising percentages of governmental revenues that go to pay military defenders of the past or future. For

indifference offered above — the counter-attractions of
more pressing tasks — do not change the fact that public
opinion in the democratic countries was not sufficiently
prepared to understand the sinister import of the return to
war economy by Germany in peace time. But it had been
a tradition of economic thinking in liberal countries
throughout the nineteenth century to pay little or no attention to the nature or effects of war, leaving that to the
militarists — a Clausewitz or a Mahan. The World War
showed that the process of destruction had become an industry; but still the tradition survived. It goes back, in
definite terms, to John Stuart Mill, writing in the years
following the Napoleonic Wars. The passage so often
quoted runs as follows: [2]

This perpetual consumption and reproduction of capital
affords the explanation of what has so often excited wonder,
the great rapidity with which countries recover from a state
of devastation; the disappearance, in a short time, of all traces
of mischiefs done by earthquakes, floods, hurricanes and the
ravages of war. An enemy lays waste a country by fire and
sword, and destroys or carries away nearly all the moveable
wealth existing in it: all the inhabitants are ruined, and yet in
a few years after, everything is much as it was before. This
vis medicatrix naturae has been a subject of sterile astonish-
ment, or has been cited to exemplify the wonderful strength
of the principle of saving, which can repair such enormous

---

the rest, social trends have apparently proceeded or halted without
being influenced by the convulsion which began twenty years ago and
which still proliferates itself in an economic convulsion of unprecedented
scope and intensity and in a series of regional political convulsions
that unhappily seem likely to coalesce. So far as the Hoover volumes
are concerned the forces unleashed in 1914 have apparently had scant
consequences in respect of habits of living, the use of leisure, or family
and social relationships.
[2] John Stuart Mill, *Political Economy*, Book I, Chapter V.

losses in so brief an interval. There is nothing at all wonderful in the matter. What the enemy have destroyed, would have been destroyed in a little time by the inhabitants themselves: the wealth which they so rapidly reproduce would have needed to be reproduced and would have been reproduced in any case, and probably in as short a time. Nothing is changed, except that during the reproduction they have not now the advantage of consuming what had been produced previously.

In other words, the economic disturbance caused by wars is but another way of using up raw materials. It is true that Mill carries us one degree from that pure obscurantism which explains post-war recovery as a result of the "curative power of nature," a formula that is a substitute for any thinking whatever on the matter, but his analysis of the "rapid repair" of the disasters which a country suffers, does not carry us much farther. According to him all depends upon energy with which the people set to work. If they have not been extirpated at the time and are not starved afterwards, they will set about rebuilding their houses and their industries in just the same way, but perhaps more quickly than in the first place.

If there is as much of food left to them or of valuables to buy food, as enables them by any amount of privation to remain alive and in working condition, they will in a short time have raised as great a produce and acquired collectively as great wealth and as great a capital as before by the mere continuance of that ordinary amount of exertion which they are accustomed to employ in their occupations. Nor does this evince any strength in the principle of saving, in the popular sense of the term, since what takes place is not intentional abstinence but involuntary privation.

Mr. Francis Hirst, in the closing pages of his volume, *The Consequences of the War to Great Britain*, recalls the fact that the professor of economics of his day at Oxford, Professor Edgeworth, carried the "optimism of the Victorians" still further in classifying this passage with those "controversies which have now lost their interest." Mr. Hirst goes on to recall that Great Britain's rapid recovery from the effects of the Napoleonic Wars, which Mill had especially in mind, left the working classes in all sections of England in a condition of terrible poverty. Above all, however, Mill left out of this picture the one outstanding cause of Britain's increasing wealth after Waterloo, the Industrial Revolution. It was not just the brawn and sinew of the population which built a new England in the Twenties and Thirties of the nineteenth century, but the steam engine and the factories and the increase of Britain's world trade as a result of them. But the mention of that revolutionary fact, to which the economists were slow to awaken, brings to mind the equally great change in the methods of production which has been taking place in these last years. The mass production of the World War was a prelude to a new industrial era in which the control of power and the need of the conversion of raw materials into articles of use gave promise of vast undreamed wealth. But as in the "hungry Forties" of the nineteenth century, the "hungry Thirties" of the twentieth offered the chilling and shocking spectacle of poverty in the midst of plenty, and impotence in place of strength.

The power of rapid recovery from the destructive effects of war, as set forth by Mill, seemed at first sight to have been demonstrated to the full by post-war Germany. As early as 1921 and 1922 it restored most of the destruction, depreciation, or impairment wrought by the War in plants and equipment, in many instances improving and modernizing the pre-war installation. Thus, the railway service which had been near collapse at the end of the War, was restored to pre-war efficiency, and the reëquipment of the railways, especially the rolling stock, was carried on during those years on a scale which later was described as "megalomania" by the Dawes Committee experts. The shortage of coal, another catastrophic aspect of the immediate post-war situation, was overcome. Vast capital development in the basic mining industries, coal and iron, on the territory of the reduced Reich, permitted the effects of both war-time developments and of subsequent territorial losses in this regard to be largely recovered. In manufacturing industries and in public utilities "productive capacity" likewise appeared restored, while in agriculture a new era of progress seemed to have been opened, thanks in part to peace-time possibilities afforded by one of the greatest technical achievements of war-time Germany, the production of synthetic nitrates.

Those developments did appear to be bearing out the notion that the costs of war are largely borne during the war, or, at any rate, that they are not shifted to a future lying beyond a rather brief period of temporary disorganization. To the extent that "productive capacity" had been preserved during the War, it seemed to be available for the service of peace-time requirements. The labor effort involved offered an opportunity of employment for those released by demobilization. And, above all, post-war developments seemed to give support to the contention, as brilliantly presented during the War by Veblen,[3] for instance, to the effect that impairment of physical wealth was of minor importance as long as the "intangible wealth" of a nation remained unaffected, — that represented

[3] Thorstein Veblen, *Imperial Germany and the Industrial Revolution*, New York, 1918.

by its mental equipment, by the "state of industrial arts," that is, the accumulated technical knowledge and the habituation of the people at large to technological processes. How misleading all this has been should be apparent from this study — or at least, from the studies and documents upon which it is based.

There is a last echo of John Stuart Mill in Sir Arthur Salter's penetrating study of European economy in 1932, "Recovery, the Second Phase." No one has had more experience with reparations and the economic problems of post-war Europe than the former head of the Financial Section of the League of Nations. This volume was written at what will probably be regarded as the decisive turning point in the history of the world when the peace machinery of the Covenant and the Kellogg Pact was being put to its first critical test in Manchuria, and Italy and Germany were on the eve of leading the world back to international anarchy. Behind it, therefore, lay the relative progress of the Twenties and no one, not even an observer so experienced as Salter, could foresee the extent of the evil days that lay ahead. Yet his volume, a sobering record of effort and failure in economic and political reconstruction, sounds this note at the beginning:

The wounds of the war were deeper than they seemed. Or rather, perhaps, they reduced the world's resistance to older weaknesses and hastened their fatal consequences. How much the least of the evils of the conflict was its material destruction! In mere production the war period bore its own burden. It made almost as much as it consumed. The human effort needed to rebuild devastated areas, or restore the fixed plant destroyed or worn out, would have been but a small toll on the world's capacity. Happily, no belligerent can utilize the production of the future; the shot fired to-day must be made yesterday,

and not to-morrow. In material resources the world was therefore not very substantially poorer in 1918 than in 1913. It had,
indeed, mortgaged the future disastrously by debts, but debts
do not enable future products to be used or wasted. They
affect only the distribution of what may be made in later years,
and — but this is much — disturb and dislocate the processes of
future production.

Careless readers of this passage have taken it as a reaffirmation of Mill's thesis because of the statement that
"in material resources the world was not very substantially
poorer in 1918 than in 1913." But the whole burden of
the paragraph is to the intent that the continuing costs in
credit and debt disturbances were far greater than those
due to the immediate destruction of the battlefield. In
short, Salter's argument was turned in the very opposite
direction from that of Mill and was not intended in support
of it. As he passed in review the economic history of the
Twenties, with its recurrent theme of recovery frustrated
when success seemed almost certain, the key to the whole
narrative lay in the fact that the destructive power of
World War economy had not yet been brought within
control. It had "mortgaged the future disastrously by
debts"; and business lives on the future. The ominous note
of the unliquidated war rang through the money markets
of the world, like the bell at Lloyd's when there is a disaster at sea. The statement, therefore, in this extract, that
"no belligerent can utilize the production of the future;
the shot fired today must be made yesterday and not to-
morrow" is only true in the most limited sense as applied to
the actual materials used, not to the work that goes into
the making, when produced under the conditions of capitalistic industry. Until the economic cost of the World
War is finally met — no one will ever be able to say exactly

when that time will come; but we know it has not come yet — some people somewhere are still making shot and shell for 1917. A simple illustration will show that this is no mere figure of speech for individuals, much less for national economies. A farmer has a barn burned down without insurance.[4] By mortgaging his farm he builds again immediately. All the physical damage is quickly repaired. But long after the carpenters have left and for years to come the farmer continues building; each bushel of wheat drives the nails of yesterday, each sacrifice of comfort buys the lumber that has been used; and, if the margin of saving is slight, the sons and daughters of the farmer may continue the work, perhaps having been denied education to prevent the creditor from seizing this embodiment of all the years of labor. From this simple illustration, it is surely clear that the material restoration of war damage is a completely misleading measure of its extent — in a world of credit.

The real difficulty in estimating war costs does not lie in such popular misconceptions as we have been dealing with, although some incautious economists have been misled by them. It lies in the fact that modern economic history has been one of cycles of good and bad times, and that any disturbance like war has to be measured against the probable trend of the subsequent period. This great law of recurring cycles, which has been traced throughout the era of capitalistic enterprise, seemed to competent observers in the late Twenties to have been set aside both by the World War on the one hand and by the great advances of modern science on the other. The dream of unlimited progress and permanent prosperity never shone with more iridescent

---

[4] The case is not different in essence with or without insurance, but is simpler if we do not have to trace the operations of credit of a great company.

hope than before the eyes of those who tried to liquidate Reparation in the Young plan. Then, when the world of affairs, instead of climbing the delectable mountains, fell into the abyss of the Great Depression, the economists whose calculations had been temporarily at fault, naturally saw in the hard times of the early Thirties the delayed and therefore intensified illustration of the truth of the cyclic law. But no upward curve of prosperity has come to reverse the downward curve of adversity, and it has been evident for some time that the explanation is that which has been implied throughout this study — that the World War had destroyed far more of the capacity of nations for buying the goods which mass production could supply than most people — there are a few exceptions — had supposed.

A short analysis of this situation was presented in my Annual Report to the Trustees of the Carnegie Endowment for International Peace in 1932, with which this study of the effects of the World War, especially upon Germany, may be brought to a close.

What the world has suffered from is not a cycle of good and bad times but an abnormality in the cycle which produced vast excesses in both prosperity and adversity. The extremes in both cases have outrun all calculations based upon the economic experience of the past; the explanation for them must therefore lie in something outside that experience. This apparently is the impact of the World War upon the structure of organized society. Nevertheless, this underlying cause has not been brought to the fore in much of the discussion concerning the economic crisis of these last years. On the contrary, the discussions have been chiefly concerned with what are in reality fallacies of the post-war period.

There is abundant excuse for this failure to think through to the basic economic effects of the War on the part of those who are studying the depression in order to find the way out, for those who shape policies must deal with the readjustment of a post-war peace-time situation. But this concentration of interest upon securing sounder present measures in finance and trade, however much it may be justified by the pressing exigencies of the hour, should not blind us to the fact that it excludes the vital and determining element from the discussion: the effect of the War upon credit. Credit is not solely a matter of finance; it depends on a basic confidence in the ordered progress of civilization. This confidence was so shaken by four years of war that many doubted if it could be rebuilt in anything like its former strength. To the surprise of the whole world, after a short interval of crisis and uncertainty, confidence returned in even larger measure than before. The surprise bred fallacies. The world of business acquired a belief in the invincible march of progress, relying upon the vastly increased capacity for production which had come about through the new industrial processes, and forgetting that the consumption market, although temporarily enlarged by the exhaustion of supplies, was fundamentally lessened by the War and its consequences. The apparent ease with which the immediate damage of the War was repaired gave an added impetus to the conception that the world of industrial credit was no longer held to the iron law of the economic cycle of prosperity and depression. The theories of economic science seemed disproved. The idea began to be advanced that the day of accounting could be indefinitely postponed by increased production, and refinanced indefinitely against still more distant futures.

The fever of speculation engendered by this superficial reading of the situation was undoubtedly a chief element in increasing the evil. Never, not even in the South Sea Bubble, was there worse gambling with fictitious values than in 1928 and 1929. But speculation alone is not a sufficient cause for the peculiar extent and depth of this depression. Fictitious values can be cleared out of the way by liquidation and, if the economic structure is sound, normal conditions begin to reassert themselves even during the period of readjustment. The real values remain, although they may be transferred in part to other hands than those of their former owners, by bank foreclosures on speculating debtors or by the purchases by conservative citizens in forced sales. Society also may profit generally from the cheaper prices of the liquidating period. Something more than speculation must be at the root of a phenomenon like that which has held the world in its grip throughout the depression years.

Post-war tariff policies have also to be borne in mind in measuring the effects of the War for they, too, are a contributing cause of the depression. It is true that not all tariffs are symbols of economic maladjustments, for some have enabled industries to make a start which ultimately proved their value in the coördinated economic life of the nation. But the tariffs of the post-war period, including our own, are of a different kind. They are frankly directed against the foreigner in order to prevent economic aggression and invasion. The whole conception is that of conflict. Every nation has been turning itself into a beleaguered city trusting for safety to its tariff walls. At last, even the classical home of free trade, England itself, yielded to the impulse. All this has happened, too, at the very moment when industry has developed mass production on a scale that cannot profitably be maintained without foreign markets.

This is the picture of the chief peace-time causes of the depression. It must be admitted that the facts present a terrible indictment against the mismanagement of capital, trade and industry. But history teaches that, even with these handicaps, the world might get along and start on its way to recovery if there were no other obstacles in its path — for it must be remembered that the world's accumulation of wealth in the past and its progress in social welfare and general prosperity were secured in the face of folly and ignorance at almost every stage of the advance. Seldom have politicians been persuaded by economists to correct their prejudices by a knowledge of economic laws. And economists, themselves, have not seldom misled the world by giving the semblance of law to the prejudices of their own time. If, in spite of all these handicaps, the application of science to power enormously increased the wealth of the world and raised the standard of living, there is no reason why the same process should not, without too long delay, have dealt with the forces of disaster now let loose upon society. In short, if the crisis of the depression was due to peace-time maladjustments, readjustment could be secured by peace-time forces, without reducing the whole world to impotence.

But what is missing in this picture? It is the first and fundamental cause which set the whole disturbance going: the World War. The sooner we realize that fact, the better we shall be prepared to apply the proper remedies. For the remedies are not merely economic; they must be political as well, and of a kind to prevent a recurrence of the cause.

It is no mere figure of speech to describe the economic depression as a part of the War. Modern war is an industry of destruction, and a world war is mass destruction which affects not only all nations but all parts of all nations. The actual fighting is but one element of the conflict. Battles are but the dramatic climax of a vast and tragic upheaval which destroys the accumulated values of society behind the lines and in quiet homes thousands of miles away from the front as effectively as the armies destroy the towns and cities in the area of the actual fighting. The blockade which ultimately brought defeat to the Central Powers affected as well the neutral world, from Holland to Argentina. It was this world-wide involvement which made the struggle of 1914–1918 unique in history, rather than the mere extent of battle lines that stretched for hundreds of miles across Europe. The first of all lessons that the World War taught was the extent of the interdependence of industrialized nations. No one before had guessed the extent of that interdependence, and even then its full import was not clearly seen, because along with the losses entailed came compensating benefits to the non-belligerents in increased prices for such goods as they were permitted to supply, and a temporary enhancement of their prosperity.

The fact which seems to have escaped adequate analysis is that modern war extends as far in time as it does in space — that it reaches out into the future even farther than over land and sea, and destroys the prosperity of years to come as well as of those gone by. When the world of modern business goes to war it mobilizes the forces of credit at the same time that it mobilizes the army and the navy. In the stress of such times the future seems illimitable, or at least it offers the chance to multiply many times over the capacities of any given moment. These potentialities of the future are sucked into the maelstrom of destruction, and this entails a much greater loss than that resulting from the actual destruction by contending armies. Warring nations mortgage their future during the period of fighting, and if the fighting continues the mortgage must be rewritten time and again, until every last item of possible recovery is thrown into the crucible. This was what happened in the four years of the World War.

Yet it is hard to keep such facts in mind, for the destruction of the future shows no visible ruins at the time of action. There is no inherent difference between the destruction of property already in our possession and property which is to be the result of future labor. But when a long period of time intervenes between the action and its consequences, so many other things may happen in the interval that we lose sight of the initial cause, or consciously endeavor to forget and to create antidotes for our misfortunes so that we may escape the otherwise inevitable effect. Although the future which the World War ravaged was a vaster field than even that great area of devastated Europe on which the actual battles were fought, nevertheless in its long reaches over the coming years of life and work, of savings and property, there were no burning cities or plundered fields, no visible sign of the presence of the destructive forces. Yet just as the "Big Berthas" of the battlefront reached out over peaceful lands to scatter their destruction at distant points, so the process of modern war reaches beyond the immediate present to scatter its ravages in distant years. The interval of peace makes the whole process seem utterly unreal — and doubly so, in this case, because the generation that fought the War did its best to forget it as soon as it possibly could.

It is this difference between the physical destruction on the battlefield or in the track of an invasion and the equally actual destruction of capital, of credits drawn against the future, which underlay so much of the disputes concerning reparations. France and Belgium could show the consequences of war and claim full reparation for the visible and obvious damage. Even in the last negotiations prior to the Lausanne Conference, there was universal assent to the claim that this kind of damage must be repaired, no matter what happened to the rest. It was the direct damage of the battlefront which remained the unconditional part of German reparations, and (as we remarked in the opening chapter of this study), anyone who has seen the desolated fields of northern France, the sites of cities leveled to deserts of mud or chalk in Flanders or Picardy, will understand why the claim was granted. But while the French of the devastated area had put their savings into houses, factories and towns which were destroyed on the spot where they stood, the people of the rest of the belligerent world contributed their material sacrifices in other ways. Some of their savings went in taxes, some in loans and patriotic contributions. The things which this money bought were never to be the property of those who paid for them, unless one thinks of safety or victory as property. They were things which no one wanted in times of peace, instruments of destruction or salvage.

By incredible effort and unlimited borrowings which gutted the edifice of credit, the War was kept going far beyond the capacity of any single generation to repay.

Almost as disastrous as the vast amount of the war debts was the effect of war financing on the investing world. The loans were presented to the purchaser not merely as patriotic contributions, but also as good investments which would bring prosperity to a nation borrowing from itself and paying itself fairly high rates of interest. Even those who expected the defeated Powers to pay the cost of the War could not expect them to pay this added profit of long-term interest-bearing debts. It is strange what fallacies were entertained in this regard, even in England. The beginning of the British national debt over two centuries ago was connected with the founding of the Bank of England, and that founding in turn was followed by the growth of Britain as the greatest banking center in the world and the center and citadel of credit before the War. All this had led to a conception of war debt as a source of revenue — which it was to those who held the title deeds to the taxes of their fellow citizens or of the citizens of other lands. Similarly, when the new debts of the World War were floated, it was strongly emphasized that they should be looked on as investments. If the amounts could have been kept within practicable limits, the difference between this kind of investment and that of capital employed in normal productive enterprises would have escaped attention. For, after all, a certain part of peace-time investments is used up in unproductive economy. But the sum total of the credits thus diverted to pay the cost of the War was far out of proportion to all others. Various calculations have been made of what the total was. None of them can be completely accurate, for it is part of the business of war financing to disguise the cost so as not to depress the fighting spirit of a nation by permitting it to know how much its reserves have been eaten into, and it is equally important not to let the enemy suspect that the sinews of war are in any way weakening. The estimate of the United States Treasury in 1928 that the net money cost to the United States was in the neighborhood of thirty-seven billion dollars needs revision now, but it gives some indication of the impact made upon a nation's reserves, an impact which was vastly increased by the demands for pensions and bonuses even when the nation no longer had the money to pay.

The theory was that all of these billions borrowed by all of the warring nations were to be paid sometime, somehow, since the loans were supposed to be for value received. The borrowing was not for future benefits but for past expenses and only a small part of those expenses could be classed as being for productive purposes. It is true that the War built up industries and by raising the standard of living democratized wealth and increased consumption. But it was, above all, an orgy of waste, and the effort which it stimulated could not be reabsorbed into normal economic processes without costly readjustment. A British economist, Dr. N. B. Dearle, has reckoned for the *Economic and Social History of the World War* that in spite of all of the work done in war-time by those who are idlers in time of peace — of which there was a vast amount — the total subtraction from England's working hours by the War was the equivalent of over three and a half million men from the first of August, 1914, to the thirty-first of

December, 1922. Upon the whole, the industry of war furnishes a productive national investment only if it can lay its burden of interest on other nations or on a future which can carry this burden by future labor. The problem is not solved by cancellation, for cancellation, either within a country or between countries, adds that much to the direct destruction of the War. By a strange fallacy, the cancellation of a war debt, especially when written off within the nation itself — as in the case of Germany, which got rid of its debt by bankruptcy — has seemed to end the history of its own war financing. The chapter seemed closed. But in reality the destruction of fluid capital which is the destruction of the power of investment, has consequences which do not terminate with the liquidation. When that capital is gone it must somehow be replaced if normal economic processes are to be restored. To replace the capital for immediate use, the future must again be mortgaged, so that in a disguised form the old war debt reappears. The destructive process of the War continues to be reflected in each new borrowing. Whether the newly borrowed funds go directly and avowedly to replace funds consumed in the orgy of waste or are connected only indirectly and disguisedly with war costs, the toll of war continues to be paid.

An additional fact disguises this process, so that it is hard to keep it clearly in our minds. As the years pass and the maturing loan obligations must be taken up, the credits for renewals must be found within the sphere of peace-time economic processes and so are not readily distinguishable from the credits for the rest of the normal functioning of business. No one, for instance, thinks today of the borrowings necessary to maintain factories, railways, or public utilities as being any continuing part of the war loans. Yet if we go deeply enough into the problem we shall find that the economic effects of the War, which continue under their various disguises in private business based on credit, are far greater in amount and far more disturbing than the direct money costs of the War which show in the balance sheets of government, even when the government has been monopolizing so much of the nation's business as was the case in wartime.

This fallacy as to war finance does not disappear with the war itself. When peace comes, the belligerent nations are so largely depleted of both supplies and the machinery of production that they momentarily stimulate industry and commerce by the market created by their vacuum. Only those nations which had their economic possibilities completely destroyed, such as Austria and Hungary, were forced to admit bankruptcy in the years immediately following the War. Even they were able to secure credits from the rest of the world to put off the day of reckoning. For the most part, the warring nations reabsorbed their armies into industry with a success which was, after all, surprising in view of the immense task which the demobilization involved and the vast readjustments of the economic life which suddenly had to be made. But this process of the return to normal peace conditions could only be attained by still further borrowing from the last source of credit left in the world. Fortunately for the time when this need arose, but unfortunately for the period following, enough of this credit was available, chiefly in the United States, to carry through the first depression of 1921, except in the case of Germany. Yet this remortgaging of the future was the undoing of the United States, for it drained this country's last resources of liquid capital for investments to make possible the reëstablishment of business throughout the world. At the height of our spending in this great enterprise of rehabilitation, we had put outside of the frontiers of the United States an equivalent of all the wealth of New England outside Massachusetts, or of a half dozen of those States which lie along the fringe of the Rocky Mountains, or of that vast empire which covers the Southwestern States of Texas, Arizona, and New Mexico. This vast export of our accumulated wealth drained the savings of more than one generation in the fallacious hope of finding profit in it for the future.

The financial evils of the post-war period were increased by the fact that we had been the profiteers of the European War prior to our entry into it. War economy is essentially wasteful, for the goods which protect life and property must be had at any cost. The United States became an arsenal for warring Europe, especially for the Entente Powers. Prices and wages reached into fabulous amounts. Thus suddenly enriched, the country was in the mood for spending, and those who never before had known the difference between stocks and bonds became speculators in a money market that was in its most dangerously speculative phase. Bankers who should have been conservative advisers of their clients became salesmen for investments of which they knew little beyond what the prospectuses told them. The fever of financial expansion distorted all sense of the fundamentals of economic life. This orgy of speculation was undoubtedly the direct cause of the panic of November, 1929, but behind it lay the continuing influence of the War showing itself in the twofold aspect of a distorted moral and economic outlook on the part of the investor, and of the destruction beyond a capacity for recovery on the part of the debtor. . . .

The conclusion is that the wealth of nations not only rests upon the healthful functioning of the economic processes, but also that the reverse holds true as well: the peace movement is a fundamental part of the economy of nations. The only solid guarantee of continuing prosperity lies in the strengthening of those instruments of international policy which are the substitutes for war: Arbitration and the World Court for the settlement of disputes, and the conference method of the League of Nations.